the
little
VIET KITCHEN

the
little
VIET KITCHEN

THUY DIEM PHAM

WITH PHOTOGRAPHY BY
DAVID LOFTUS

A.

Introduction

Me, aged 3,
in front of
grandma's house.
The photo was
taken to send to
London for dad.
1985, Cầu Ngang,
Vietnam.

The ground was always warm; at midday it was unbearable to walk outside the house. The sandy roads were so hot on my little feet but I had to save my slippers for special occasions. Dad had sent them in a big paper box all the way from England! They were so special to me and I wanted them to be perfect for the day I would 'meet him'. I was never really sure what he looked like as he'd left for England when I was only three years old, but no one would have guessed that considering how often and how proudly I spoke about him to the other school kids. I spoke of him often, despite not really knowing him at all. Talking about him brought hope for my sister me, and a little comfort for my mother.

I had no idea what London promised, but even at a young age, I understood that we needed to leave the farm if we wanted a chance at a proper education and successful career. If I'm honest, I was a little confused as I was very happy, but often saw mum crying at night. At the time, I could only assume she missed dad. All I knew was that dad had to leave to seek a better life for us, risking his own at sea, with no guarantee of success or return to his home country. These are the sacrifices a father makes for his children, and for that I will always be indebted to him.

However, staying in Vietnam was by no means any less of a sacrifice on my mother's part. Having two children and the farm — and no husband around — meant that she played two roles. But a mother's love for her children is never measurable; she did everything in her power to keep us safe and happy. No words can fully describe a mother's love. Mum made selfless decisions and sacrifices without regret. She kept her dreams at bay to protect her children from harm and the reality of life with little — yet love in abundance. She has made me the tough woman I am today.

My mum showed us love in many ways. When extravagant gifts were not an option, she expressed them through the dishes she put on the table for her family. The ingredients may not have been sophisticated, nor presented too luxuriously, but oh my, the smell of those delicious home cooked Vietnamese treats always let me know how much my mummy loved me and my siblings. She cooked with creativity, modesty and love. She stayed strong like it was her duty, loved like it was a blessing and lived to pave the way for her children.

My grandparents took us in for a while, as we were made homeless very soon after dad left. I've been told the house is never quiet when I'm around; so I can only assume I was a delight to their home! Mum's parents could not afford to feed an extra three mouths, but they would never turn us away, and if anything were secretly happy to have mum home again.

Eventually mum found a new home for us, but every few days she would make the six-hour journey north to Saigon to sell food on the streets. On these days she would get home very late and so my sister and I would stay at our grandparents' house. I always loved our visits there. They owned a small rice farm and had what seemed to me a huge house, although in reality it was just a single room about

My big sister Mỹ Hạnh and me in our New Years outfits, made by mum, with our brand new shoes! We don't look happy but I promise we were over the moon, if not just a little scared of the big man with the camera. 1986, Cầu Ngang, Vietnam.

Me, 3 years old, with my big sister and mummy, posing somewhat awkwardly for a photo to send to dad. This was the first photo we sent him; we weren't sure it would even get to him, but we were hopeful. 1984, Trà Vinh, Vietnam.

the size of a large living room in the UK with blankets hanging down to make separate rooms. They had a garden with lots of fruit trees — coconuts, mangoes, bananas, guavas, Vietnamese cherries, sugar-apples and rose-apples, amongst others. They had lemongrass and Thai basil growing everywhere and even a rag tag collection of scrawny farm animals grazing randomly around the garden. And most importantly, they always had something cooking in the kitchen that smelled amazing.

The contrast of being often surrounded by food and yet not always having enough for dinner is, I think, where my deep love and respect for food really began. Plus I've always had a bottomless appetite so have spent my whole life either eating, or thinking about what I'll be eating next!

On those days at the farm I would constantly follow grandma around trying to be helpful with the daily chores. Looking back on it I'm sure that I was more of a hindrance than a help, but at the time I was certain I was an essential assistant that she couldn't possibly manage without. Grandma always looked and sounded angry, yet had a kind and mischievous glint in her eyes. After the chores were done she would call me over to her and I would run as fast as I could because I knew what that meant — it was always delicious! She would wear a well-worn, patchwork áo bà ba, a traditional Vietnamese shirt, worn by both men and women in the rural areas of the Mekong Delta. It had two small pockets on the front, and as if by magic, sweet treats would appear from them! Normally this was either kẹo dừa, a coconut caramel wrapped in rice paper, or kẹo mè xửng, a brittle sesame candy. My favourite though, was me ngào đường, a deliciously chewy tamarind sweet. I guess it could probably be considered a fairly meagre payment for a day's work on the farm, but I was very happy with the deal then and I'd probably be tempted by it again today!

At the time, what I really wanted was to be an adult, as that way I'd be allowed to help with the cooking rather than just the cleaning or the other chores around the farm. However, it was more likely because I thought once I'd learned to cook I'd be able to eat all the time!

My memories of my grandpa are different. Whilst grandma never stopped moving and did everything at a frightening

pace, grandpa was the complete opposite. He would always
sit on the front porch sipping on tea, often alone unless
guests came. He wouldn't say much, often nothing at all.
Calm, kind and wise-looking, he rarely smiled or laughed.
Everyone seemed to fear grandpa but I never understood
why. Looking back as an adult I can see that actually the
people of our village just had an incredible respect for
him — but that was something I couldn't understand at that
young age. I sometimes sat with him to keep him company,
but grandma would always shoo me away saying 'you can't sit
there. Go outside and play.' This would puzzle me because
surely he wanted company and who better than his favourite
granddaughter?! I would constantly ask him questions as
there seemed so much to learn about being a grown up and he
always seemed to have all of the answers!

I would not have wanted to grow up any other way. My fondest
memories were on the farm, with grandma and grandpa always
in the picture. Even when they were not next to me, I always
felt loved and safe, knowing they were there. They are part
of who I am today, though maybe they don't know it. Grandma,
the traditional Vietnamese wife and mother,
and grandpa who was kind-hearted and full of
wisdom and life lessons to pass on.

Me and my big
sister in our
brand new dresses
sent all the
way from exotic
London! 1985, Trà
Vinh, Vietnam.

Walks to my great-grandma's house were
always something I looked forward to. The
route was lined with yet more fruit trees
and we'd pick all the hanging fruits along
the way. New ones would ripen every day so
there'd usually be enough to fill even my
belly. Great-grandma had treats too, of
course. She would keep them in the tall,
wooden, fancy French cupboard that no one
was allowed to touch and they were reserved
only for when we did well at school. It
seems that no matter where in the world
you're from, grandmas and great-grandmas
always know the best ways to motivate you!

In her special French cupboard she also
had beautiful sets of china that were never
used, they just sat behind the glass to be
looked at. She would polish them every day
without fail and knew every tiny detail on
them. My sister and I were so scared of
breaking them that we wouldn't even dare to
go close to the cupboard! I always wondered
if she would ever use them; it seemed silly
just to let them sit there whilst we drank

out of old metal or plastic mugs. I remember asking her why one day, knowing there was a good chance of being told off for being nosy. She smiled, patted me on the head and cryptically said 'one day you will understand'.

These beautiful plates are now by my side, and yes I do understand, great-grandma. They had once belonged to great-grandpa's grandparents and after a mine killed him during the war, they were all she had to remind her of him. There were no such things as cameras for farmers like them; they were only for the rich folk in the city. Instead, they would just have a picture drawn by an artist when they were about 50 years old and that would be placed on their altar when they died. So little keepsakes like these old teapots and plates would take on so much more value than their actual worth and become heirlooms to pass down through the generations. So whilst they were her reminders of great-grandpa, they were also her inheritance and it was her duty to keep them pristine so she could pass them on to the next generation.

I truly love having this small piece of my Vietnamese heritage with me here in England and I hope that my great-great-great-grandma would have been happy to see them in the photos in the pages of this book. I know that grandma will.

When I was young and still living in Vietnam, I didn't really understand the situation my family was in, but I knew my father had gone away to find a home for us with lots of food and a big school, where we could have lots of pencils and paper. And really, that was all I ever really wanted — enough food so I wouldn't be hungry and enough pencils that I didn't have to worry if I lost mine. The last time I lost it I didn't go home after school: I knew that mum would be so mad as I wouldn't be allowed to go to school without it and she couldn't afford to buy a new one. So I ran the two miles to auntie #2's house in tears, hoping that she would somehow be able to magic one up and make everything OK without mum finding out. Thankfully she bought me a new pencil and promised not to tell. She kept her word and mum only found out many years later. This meant that I only got a stern look rather than the real telling off that the five-year-old me really dreaded. To this day, every time I misplace a pen or a pencil a little kick of fear hits me, reminding me to be grateful for what we have and to never take anything for granted, even the simplest or most basic of things.

When you have so little, everything means so much. I sometimes wonder how much of who I am today is down to where

I came from, how strong my family role-models were and how hard we all worked just to put food on the table. My love for food comes so naturally, I feel it in my bones. I am not alone in this either; my whole region of Vietnam (and probably the whole country) has so much love and respect for food.

I have always channelled that respect for ingredients into cooking. Creating dishes both traditional and new has been a lifelong hobby and I count myself very lucky that it has also now become my job! I am so happy that I have this opportunity to present some of these dishes to you. I hope that you cook many of them in your own homes and that they bring you and your family and friends all the joy that they bring to me.

The day before flying to London! We were so excited as the day we'd been looking forward to for years was finally here, but also unbearably nervous now it was! 1989, Sài Gòn Zoo, Vietnam.

Vietnamese Food Culture

Food plays a huge part of life in Vietnam and stretching back centuries it has been the backbone of our culture and way of life. It is used to this day in many ways, from welcoming friends into your home, to expressing love for someone, either romantically or familial. It is therefore not surprising that the three meals a day are something set in stone and very important in people's day to day life. In a country where people have so little in terms of possessions, so much more emphasis and meaning is put on the role of food and of the family: the two constants that everyone has in common.

It is still generally the case that the women are the chefs and the men go out to work bringing in the money to feed the family. All over Vietnam, but especially in the rural areas, work starts in the very early hours of the morning, which explains why the traditional Vietnamese breakfast is so hearty. Generally it consists of pho noodle soup, hủ tiếu noodle soup or a rice porridge with deep fried doughnuts, all being served with meat and plenty of slow burning carbohydrates. Energy has to be stored for a long day of work on the farm or in other labour-intensive jobs with a long wait until lunch, often in 40 degrees heat!

Dinner is still considered special in Vietnam as it's the one time the whole family sits down at the table and enjoys a meal together. When I was growing up mobile phones didn't exist and even if you were lucky enough to have a TV, then generally the only programmes on were Vietnamese opera or propaganda, so there were none of the distractions we have these days. That being said, maybe it had nothing to do with that and it's simply that I love my food so much, but either way, I find that most of my fond childhood memories are connected to food. We may not have had much to eat, but oh my, what we had was tasty!

Until the introduction of crop boosting chemicals and pesticides in the 1970s, the food in Vietnam was all organic. Fortunately there is a large and growing movement from both the general population and the government to get back to that now and many farmers all across the country are switching back to traditional methods of crop production as a result. My grandpa steadfastly refused to ever use them, however, always being suspicious of the safety aspects, and preferred to keep his rice production at a natural level than take the risk of long-term contamination of his fields. As a result, from as far back as I can remember, I have had the virtues of organic food impressed upon me and this is something I have always maintained at home and I have implemented where possible in my restaurant too. I remember that every time we had something to celebrate, grandma would head out into the yard and stand for a while looking at the chickens before selecting one, saying 'it's your time today little one'. Then two hours later it would be on the table, which is as organic as it gets really.

Traditionally, a Vietnamese family meal would be a shared one, with rice being the mandatory staple, served in individual bowls in front of each person. A variety of dishes to complement the rice would be placed in the centre of the table, in easy reach of everyone at the meal. Often a variation of styles and flavours would be present: a salty meat dish such as thịt khô trứng (page 42), a vegetable stir-fry like rau muống xào tỏi (page 165) and a clear soup such as khổ qua nhồi thịt heo (page 72) to balance the meal. Small side dishes of fresh herbs, dipping sauces, dried or cured fish or pickles would normally be added to the table too.

Growing up in a large family, my dad having twelve siblings and mum eight, whenever it came to family meals there were so many rules and matters of dining etiquette to be observed that as a curious and ever-hungry child, it became quite confusing. Why is grandpa having his rice served first when he doesn't even look hungry? I'd already told mum I was starving so had to come to the conclusion that grown-ups simply never listened. Fairly obviously it turned out that is a simple act of respect for elders, and the head of the family would be served rice first. Followed by uncles, aunties then children, all generally in age order.

When passing things to people, especially someone older, you should always use both hands. Until this day, I naturally still do this as I can hear grandpa's voice reminding us grandchildren that it shows respect and must be done at all times, not just at family meals. This was even more important when we had guests or were visiting others, as it would reflect badly on the elders if we didn't.

Another rule that used to confuse me a little was the rice level. It should always be three-quarters full, as a full bowl of rice should only be served on the alter, to the ancestors. To me it just meant that I would have to ask for my second portion sooner so seemed a little inefficient. However, when dad wisely suggested that it gave more room to pile the delicious meat and vegetables into our bowls it suddenly sounded a lot more reasonable to the greedy little me! Although he never had a convincing argument as to why I couldn't just have a bigger bowl…

One of the slightly less obvious rules was that the person serving the rice should always be the youngest daughter-in-law of the family. Sounds a little like a bad deal for her but it is also tradition that she, along with her husband, of course, will inherit the house and the family land when the parents pass away. I used to think poor auntie, by the time she is done there will be no food left! But now I can see it's not such a bad deal after all. A tradition that actually has a strategy plan to say the least.

There are many forms of table etiquette to remember if you don't want to be disrespectful to your hosts. Things such as: always selecting with your eyes before using your chopsticks to avoid tossing food around in search of the piece you want; always bringing food to your bowl before eating, never taking straight from the serving plates in the centre of the table; never placing your chopsticks vertically on your rice bowl, as again this is exclusively for when you place food on the altar for the ancestors; and as tempting as it is, not just eating all the best bits and expensive meats, as being thoughtful and considerate to the other diners is essential. Always remember that you are sharing so it is courteous to think of others.

Wasting food is considered very disrespectful and a huge insult to the cook. Whilst this is partly down to the monetary aspect of course, a lot of Vietnamese ingredients are fresh and inexpensive, especially when picked from the garden, so it is more about the time and effort put into creating the dish. In Vietnamese cooking, the heart and soul that goes into creating a meal can be tasted in every bite. The chef has been stood in the kitchen all day to make that broth, so never take what you can't finish. If you don't think you can struggle through that bowl… Well suck it up and keep going! The cook can't take back that eight hours so show them respect and eat it all. As you can imagine, this has never been an issue for me!

Chilli and Lemongrass Marinade

Sốt Sa Tế

For this marinade, as with most of the recipes in this chapter, I've suggested quantities to make a largish amount, but you can scale it to suit your needs.

Soak the dried shrimp for 30 minutes in a bowl of warm water. Drain, pat dry with paper towels, then blitz in a food processor for 30 seconds to form a fine floss and set aside.

Heat the oil in a saucepan over a medium heat until it reaches 160°C. An easy way to tell when the oil is ready is to place a wooden chopstick into it – when bubbles form on the surface of the oil it is ready.

Add the garlic and the white parts of the spring onions, and fry for 1–2 minutes, or until the garlic starts to turn light golden in colour. Add the dried shrimp and shrimp paste to the pan and stir in the chilli flakes, sugar, salt and fish sauce. Reduce the heat to very low and cook for a further 20 minutes, stirring occasionally to stop the sugar from burning.

Pour in the chilli oil and continue to cook for 5 minutes.

Take the pan off the heat and leave the marinade to cool overnight, uncovered. Transfer to an airtight container or jar and pour over enough oil to cover the marinade mixture.

Makes approx 600ml

200g dried shrimp
500ml vegetable oil
2 tablespoons finely diced garlic
10 spring onions, white parts only, finely chopped
1 tablespoon shrimp paste
1 teaspoon dried red chilli flakes
2 tablespoons granulated sugar
1 teaspoon salt
2 teaspoons fish sauce
200ml chilli oil
vegetable oil

Pho Spice Rub

Gia Vị Phở

Place all ingredients into a spice grinder and blitz for 1 minute. Transfer to a jar and store in a cool, dry larder for up to 6 months.

Makes 150g

50g star anise
50g cinnamon stick
30g coriander seeds
10 fennel seeds
5 cloves
5 cardamom pods

Annatto Seed Oil

Dầu Hạt Điều

Annatto seeds can be found in speciality Turkish or Indian stores, or any good Asian grocers. These beautiful seeds are natural colouring used for staining or colouring dishes, but can also be used as a spice. For an amazing and delicious kick try adding dried red chillies.

Heat the oil in a saucepan over a low heat until it reaches 160°C. An easy way to tell when the oil is ready is to place a wooden chopstick into it – when bubbles form on the surface of the oil it is ready.

Add the seeds and fry for 15–20 minutes, until the oil has turned dark red in colour. Keep an eye on the oil, making sure to take the pan off the heat before the seeds blacken and burn (this will result in a bitter, burnt flavour).

Leave to cool for 3 hours, then pour into a jar. Allow the oil to settle overnight, uncovered. Most people will tell you to strain the seeds from the oil but I prefer to leave them in. The seeds will fall to the bottom of the jar and really intensify the flavour of the oil in the following weeks as it sits on your larder shelf. The oil will keep for 12 months at room temperature.

Makes 500ml

500ml vegetable oil
5 tablespoons annatto seeds

Spring Onion Oil

Mỡ Hành

Heat the oil in a saucepan over a medium heat until it reaches 160°C. An easy way to tell when the oil is ready is to place a wooden chopstick into it – when bubbles form on the surface of the oil it is ready.

Add the shallots and the white parts of the spring onions, and fry for 2 minutes. Add the fish sauce followed by the green parts of the spring onions, and fry for a further minute. Take the pan off the heat and leave to cool completely before transferring to an airtight jar. This oil will keep for up to 4 weeks in the fridge as long as the level of oil is above the spring onions.

Makes 400ml

125ml vegetable oil
2 Asian shallots, peeled and
   sliced
250g spring onions, finely
   sliced, white and green parts
   separated
1 tablespoon fish sauce

Pickled Mustard Cabbage

Cải Bẹ Xanh Muối

Mix all the ingredients together well in a large bowl and either eat immediately for a bitter, mustard flavour with a crunchy texture, or leave overnight for a more sour pickle taste.

Keeps for 4–5 days in the fridge. (See page 40–41 for an image.)

Makes 300g

300g mustard cabbage, woody parts removed and discarded, sliced into 5cm lengths
10g ginger, finely sliced into matchsticks
1 teaspoon finely diced garlic
1 tablespoon finely chopped Asian shallots
juice of ½ lime
1 tablespoon granulated sugar
1 teaspoon fish sauce

Pickled Carrot and Daikon

Củ Cải Và Cà Rốt Ngâm Chua

Heat the rice vinegar and sugar in a saucepan over a medium heat, stirring until all the sugar has dissolved. Take off the heat and leave to cool completely.

Put the carrots and daikon in a jar, then pour over the cooled vinegar mixture. Seal the jar with a lid and place in the fridge for at least a day and up to 5 days to pickle.

Makes enough to fill a 500ml jar

250ml rice vinegar
250g granulated sugar
250g carrots, cut into fine matchsticks
250g daikon, cut into fine matchsticks

Soy-cured Duck Egg Yolks

Trứng Vịt Ngâm Nước Tương

Add the sugar to the warm water to a bowl and stir until dissolved. Crush the lemongrass and add it to the bowl, then leave to cool completely for 30 minutes. Add the soy sauce and stir well.

Separate one of the duck egg yolks from the whites. Do this by cracking the egg carefully and gently dropping it into the palm of your hand. Spread your fingers just enough to allow the whites to pass through into a small bowl. Gently pass the yolk between your hands until all of the whites have fallen away (discard the whites), then place the yolk directly into the bowl with the soy sauce marinade. Check to make sure the bowl of yolks doesn't have any small pieces of shell in it and carefully remove if so.

Repeat the process for the other eggs, then leave in the fridge for 3 hours to cure. Take the cured yolks out of the fridge at least 1 hour before serving to bring them up to room temperature.

If you want the yolks to be firmer and less runny, simply leave them to cure for longer. The yolks will thicken to a more gelatine-like texture and have a more intense flavour. (See page 196–197 for an image.)

Serves 6

2 tablespoons caster sugar
300ml warm water
1 lemongrass stalk
300ml soy sauce
6 duck eggs

Soy-braised Shiitake Mushrooms

Nấm Đông Cô Ngâm Nước Tương

Soak the shiitake mushrooms in a bowl of warm water for 10 minutes until they are fully saturated and soft. Gently squeeze away the excess water.

Heat the oil in a large frying pan over a medium heat to 160°C. An easy way to tell when the oil is ready is to place a wooden chopstick into it – when bubbles form on the surface of the oil it is ready.

Add the shiitake mushrooms and stir-fry for a minute until they are a lovely golden colour all over. Add the garlic and ginger and continue to stir-fry for a further minute.

Carefully pour in 125ml of water, add the soy sauce, sugar and crushed black peppercorns and reduce the heat to a simmer for 10 minutes.

Allow to cool for 10 minutes before placing in an airtight container or jar and refrigerating. These will keep for a couple of months as long as the liquid level is above the mushrooms.

Makes 250g

250g dried shiitake mushrooms
3 tablespoons vegetable oil
1 tablespoon finely diced garlic
25g ginger, cut into fine
   matchsticks
1 tablespoon soy sauce
1 tablespoon granulated sugar
1 teaspoon crushed black
   peppercorns

Deep-fried Tofu

Đậu Hũ Chiên

Take the tofu out of its packaging, drain and wrap in a clean tea towel. Place on a chopping board and put a baking tray and something heavy (such as a few tins) on top of the tofu to weigh it down. Leave this unusual looking set-up in place for 1 hour to drain the water from the tofu, then cut into 4 even pieces.

Heat the oil in a saucepan over a medium heat until it reaches 160°C. An easy way to tell when the oil is ready is to place a wooden chopstick into it – when bubbles form on the surface of the oil it is ready.

Add the tofu pieces to the oil and deep-fry for 3 minutes. Flip the tofu over and continue to deep-fry for a further 3 minutes, until nicely golden all over.

Use a slotted spoon to remove the tofu pieces from the pan. Drain on paper towels and allow to cool.

Cut the tofu pieces into 5cm × 1cm thick strips. If storing, set aside until completely cool and put into an airtight container. The tofu will keep for up to 3 days in the fridge.

Makes 400g

400g firm tofu, preferably organic tofu
500ml vegetable oil

Crispy Fried Shallots

Hành Tím Phi Khô

Making a large batch of crispy fried shallots may be time consuming but in one sitting you can fry up enough to last a month. Or of course whatever amount you have time for — this recipe is easily scaled according to what you need, just make sure you have plenty of oil to fry the shallots in.

Heat the oil in a large deep-frying pan over the lowest heat for around 15 minutes. An easy way to tell when the oil is ready is to place a wooden chopstick into it – when bubbles form on the surface of the oil it is ready.

Add the shallots in batches of around 200g, and deep-fry until golden brown. Remove the shallots with a slotted spoon and drain on paper towels. Repeat this process until all of the shallots are cooked, then leave them on the paper towels overnight. Allowing the shallots to air-dry will help to preserve them. Transfer to an airtight container where they will keep for up to 1 month.

Makes a lot, but use them to add crunch to any dish

2 litres vegetable oil
2kg Asian shallots, peeled and very finely chopped

Crispy Garlic

Tỏi Chiên Giòn

Heat the oil in a saucepan over a low heat until it reaches 140°C. An easy way to tell when the oil is ready is to place a wooden chopstick into it – when bubbles form on the surface of the oil it is ready.

Add the garlic and fry for 1–2 minutes, until the garlic turns light golden in colour. Immediately remove the garlic using a slotted spoon and drain on paper towels for 1 hour. Transfer to an airtight container and store in a cool, dry larder.

Makes 25g

250ml vegetable oil
6 garlic cloves, finely sliced

Confit Shallots

Hành Phi

Heat the oil in a saucepan over a medium heat until it reaches 160°C. An easy way to tell when the oil is ready is to place a wooden chopstick into it – when bubbles form on the surface of the oil it is ready. Put the annatto seeds in a spice strainer and add to the oil for 1 minute; the oil will turn a lovely dark red and be infused with the intense flavour of the annatto seeds. Immediately lower the heat and remove the spice strainer with the annatto seeds.

Add the shallots, and fry for 10–15 minutes until lovely and golden. Remove from the heat and allow to cool completely before transferring to a jar and leaving to sit overnight with the lid off. Store at room temperature.

Makes 500g

250ml vegetable oil
2 tablespoons annatto seeds
500g Asian shallots, peeled

Roasted Peanuts

Đậu Phộng Nướng

Preheat the oven to 160°C/140°C Fan/Gas Mark 3.

Divide the peanuts between two non-stick roasting trays or trays lined with baking paper, spreading them out evenly in the trays. Place the trays in the oven and roast the peanuts for 15 minutes, then remove and give them a shake or give them a stir to ensure even roasting. Return to the oven for a further 10 minutes, until the peanuts are a lovely golden colour. Remove and leave to cool for 3 hours. Store in an airtight jar at room temperature for up to 3 months.

Makes 1kg

1kg unsalted blanched peanuts

Salt, Pepper and Lime Dip

Muối Tiêu Chanh

This is a great dip for any seafood dish. You make it as and when you need it because it doesn't keep.

Mix all the ingredients together well in a small bowl.

Makes approx 40g

25g black peppercorns, crushed
15g salt
juice of ½ lime

Caramel Sauce

Nước Màu

Heat the sugar and 125ml of water in a saucepan over a medium heat. Stir slowly, until the sugar has completely dissolved. Reduce the heat to low and cook for 10 minutes until the mixture starts to smoke and caramelise, then carefully pour in another 125ml of water (be super careful at this point as adding the water will cause the hot sugar to splutter) and stir until fully combined. Continue to cook for a further 5 minutes, until the mixture starts to smoke once more and is a rich dark reddish black colour, then take off the heat and pour into a heatproof jar. Set aside to cool and rinse the pan while still hot to make it easy to clean.

Keeps indefinitely at room temperature.

Makes 300ml

500g granulated sugar

Creamy Coconut Custard

Nước Cốt Dừa

Nước cốt dừa is a classic custard topping used on many traditional Vietnamese desserts. It adds a savoury twist to any sweet dish, a Vietnamese signature.

Heat the coconut cream, salt, sugar and cornflour in a saucepan over a medium heat, and stir continuously while bringing the mixture to the boil. As soon as it thickens to the consistency of double cream, take the pan off the heat. If serving right away, sprinkle with toasted sesame seeds.

Set the custard aside to cool completely, then transfer to an airtight container or jar and store in the fridge for up to 5 days.

Makes 400ml

400ml coconut cream
½ teaspoon salt
1 tablespoon granulated sugar
2 teaspoons cornflour
1 tablespoon toasted sesame
   seeds (optional)

Fish Sauce and Lime Salad Dressing

Nước Mắm Trộn Gỏi

The recipe for this dressing, as well as those on the following pages, makes a large quantity, which might seem a little daunting. However, we use it as a dressing or dipping sauce for so many of our dishes that it really is worth making a large quantity and keeping it in the fridge for a couple of months. Otherwise, you can scale the ingredients by a half or quarter to get a smaller amount to suit your needs.

Put the lime juice, crushed rock sugar and fish sauce into a small saucepan and set over a medium heat to dissolve the sugar. As soon as the sugar has melted, turn off the heat and set aside to cool down.

When completely cooled, add the garlic and chillies and mix well. This dressing can be stored in the fridge for up to 3 months.

Makes approx 1 litre

500ml lime juice
1.2kg rock sugar, crushed
250ml fish sauce
16 garlic cloves, finely diced
8 red chillies (or to taste), finely diced

Classic Fish Dipping Sauce

Nước Mắm Chấm

Put the lime juice, crushed rock sugar, fish sauce and 500ml of water into a small saucepan and set over a medium heat to dissolve the sugar. As soon as the sugar has melted, turn off the heat and leave set aside to cool down.

When completely cooled, add the garlic and chillies, and mix well. This dipping sauce can be stored in the fridge for up to 3 months.

Makes approx 1 litre

250ml lime juice
600g rock sugar, crushed
250ml fish sauce
16 garlic cloves, finely diced
8 red chillies (or to taste), finely diced

Tamarind Fish Sauce

Nước Mắm Me

Put the tamarind paste, crushed rock sugar, fish sauce and 60ml of water into a small saucepan and set over a medium heat to dissolve the sugar. As soon as the sugar has melted, turn off the heat and set aside to cool down.

When completely cooled, add the garlic and chillies, and mix well. The sauce can be stored in the fridge for up to 3 months.

Makes 300ml

100g tamarind paste
150g rock sugar, crushed
45ml fish sauce
4 fat garlic cloves, finely diced
2 red chillies, finely diced

Ginger Fish Sauce

Nước Mắm Gừng

Put the lime juice, crushed rock sugar and fish sauce into a small saucepan and set over a medium heat to dissolve the sugar. As soon as the sugar has melted, turn off the heat and leave on the side to cool down.

When completely cooled, add the garlic, chillies and ginger, and mix well. The sauce can be stored in the fridge for up to 3 months.

Makes 1.4 litres

250ml lime juice
50g rock sugar, crushed
750ml fish sauce
16 fat garlic cloves, finely diced
8 red chillies, finely diced
320g ginger, finely diced

Pineapple Fish Sauce

Nước Mắm Khóm

Put the lemon juice, fish sauce and sugar into a small saucepan and set over a medium heat. Stir until the sugar has dissolved. Immediately take the pan off the heat and set the sauce aside to cool completely.

Stir in the garlic, pineapple and chillies, and mix well. The sauce can be stored for up to 3 months in the fridge.

Makes approx 2 litres

500ml lemon juice
750ml fish sauce
600g rock sugar, crushed
8 garlic cloves, finely diced
600g finely chopped pineapple
8 red chillies (or to taste), finely
   chopped

Vegan Soy Dipping Sauce

Nước Tương Chay

Put the lime juice, rock sugar, soy sauce and 500ml of water into a small saucepan and set over a medium heat. Stir until the sugar has dissolved. Immediately take the pan off the heat and set the sauce aside to cool completely.

Stir in the garlic and chillies, and mix well. The sauce can be stored for up to 3 months in the fridge.

Makes approx 1.5 litres

250ml lime juice
600g rock sugar, crushed
250ml soy sauce
16 fat garlic cloves, finely diced
8 red chillies (or to taste), finely
    diced

Soy and Lemongrass Sauce

Nước Tương Sả Ớt

Put the lemon juice, crushed rock sugar and soy sauce into a small saucepan and set over a medium heat to dissolve the sugar. As soon as the sugar has melted, turn off the heat and set aside to side to cool down.

When completely cooled, add the garlic, lemongrass and chillies, and mix well. The sauce can be stored for up to 3 months in the fridge.

Makes 500ml

250ml lemon juice
600g rock sugar, finely crushed
500ml soy sauce
8 fat garlic cloves, finely diced
3 lemongrass stalks, finely diced
8 red chillies (or to taste), finely
    diced

Mayonnaise

Sốt Mayonnaise

In a large bowl, whisk the egg yolks and very gradually add 250ml of the oil, whisking until the mixture has thickened. This will take 5 minutes if whisking by hand but you could also use a stick blender.

Whisk in the vinegar, salt and lemon juice, then gradually pour in the remaining oil, whisking all the time until the mixture has once again thickened. The mayonnaise can be eaten immediately or stored for up to 1 week in an airtight jar in the fridge.

Makes 500ml

3 free-range egg yolks
500ml vegetable oil
1 tablespoon rice vinegar
pinch of salt
juice of ½ lemon

Plum and Peanut Sauce

Tương Ớt To Đậu Phộng

In a small saucepan over a medium heat, heat the vegetable oil and garlic and leave until the garlic is a little brown in colour.

Add the rest of the ingredients, except the peanuts, and stir well. Leave for 2–3 minutes. When you see little bubbles appear give it one final stir and remove from the heat.

When completely cooled, transfer to an airtight container and store for up to 5 days. When you want to serve, give a sprinkle with the peanuts.

Makes 75–80ml

2 tablespoons vegetable oil
3 fat garlic cloves, finely diced
2 bird's eye chillies, finely diced
2 tablespoons sweet chilli sauce,
    or 1 tablespoon sriracha chilli
    sauce
4 tablespoons hoisin sauce
2 teaspoons granulated sugar
1 tablespoon salted roasted
    peanuts, crushed

Tomato Sauce

Nước Sốt Cà Chua

Heat the oil in a saucepan over a medium heat. When hot, add the garlic and stir-fry for 1–2 minutes, until golden.

Add the tomatoes and the coconut water, and stir-fry for a further 5 minutes. Season with the sugar and salt, and reduce the heat to low. Simmer until the sauce has a lovely thick texture, about the consistency of a good marinara sauce.

Take off the heat and leave to cool. Transfer to an airtight jar or container where it will keep for 5 days in the fridge.

Makes 300ml

1 tablespoon vegetable oil
2 garlic cloves, diced
250g ripe plum tomatoes, seeds
    removed and diced
125ml coconut water
1 tablespoon granulated sugar
1 teaspoon salt

Chicken Stock

Canh Gà

Preheat the oven to 180°C/160°C Fan/Gas Mark 4.

Place the onions and ginger on a roasting tray and roast for 25 minutes. Remove and leave to cool for 10 minutes. Peel away the outside layer of the onions and use a vegetable peeler to peel the ginger. Set aside.

Fill a stockpot with 4 litres of water and set over a high heat. Bring to the boil, add the chicken and boil for 3 minutes. Take the pot off the heat, drain away the water, clean the pot and rinse the chicken under cold running water.

Return the chicken to the pot along with the roasted onions and ginger, salt, fish sauce and crushed rock sugar. Pour in 4 litres of water, ensuring it's a clear 2.5cm above the ingredients in the pot. Set over a high heat and bring the water to the boil. Skim off any impurities from the surface, cover with a lid, leaving a finger-width gap for the steam to escape, and lower the heat. Simmer for 4 hours, checking on the stock every hour, removing impurities from the surface as necessary.

Remove the pot from the heat, take out the chicken and leave to sit on a chopping board. Take out the onions and ginger and skim off any impurities floating on the surface of the stock. Leave the stock to settle for 2 hours.

Strain the stock through a fine sieve into a large container, making sure to stop when you get close to the bottom of the pot as this will consist of mainly gritty residue from the flavouring ingredients.

Allow to cool completely, then store in the fridge for up to 3 days or freeze for up to 3 months.

Lastly, strip all of the meat from the chicken. There's no point in wasting it! After being simmered for 4 hours in your broth, the flesh will be so soft and moist and perfect for any number of recipes, such as the chicken rice porridge (page 63) or the chicken and mango salad (page 174).

Makes 2 litres

2 onions, skins on
100g ginger
1 whole chicken, 1.5–2kg
1 tablespoon salt
1 tablespoon fish sauce
200g rock sugar, crushed

Beef Stock

Canh Bò

Preheat the oven to 180°C/160°C Fan/Gas Mark 4.

Place the onions and ginger in a roasting tray and roast for 25 minutes. Remove and leave to cool for 10 minutes. Peel away the outside layer of the onions and the ginger and set aside.

Fill a stockpot with 4 litres of water and set over a high heat. Bring to the boil, add the bone marrow, shank bones and oxtail, and boil for 3 minutes. Take the pot off the heat, drain away the water, clean the pot and rinse the bones and oxtail under cold running water.

Return the oxtail and bones to the pot along with the roasted onions and ginger, the daikon, salt, fish sauce and crushed rock sugar. Pour in 4 litres of water, ensuring it's a clear 2.5cm above the ingredients in the pot. Set over a high heat and bring the water to the boil. Skim off any impurities from the surface, cover with a lid, leaving a finger-width gap for the steam to escape, and lower the heat. Simmer the stock for 3 hours, checking every hour to remove any impurities from the surface as necessary.

Put the spices into a muslin and secure with kitchen string. Add to the pot and continue to simmer the stock for a further 2 hours. Take out the large ingredients, and the bag of spices and skim off any impurities floating on the surface of the stock. Leave on the side to cool and settle for 2 hours.

Strain the stock through a fine sieve into a large container, making sure to stop when you get close to the bottom of the pot as this will consist of mainly gritty residue from the flavouring ingredients.

Allow to cool completely, then store in the fridge for up to 3 days or freeze for up to 3 months.

Makes 2 litres

2 onions, skin on
200g ginger
1kg bone marrow
1kg beef shank bones
1kg oxtail
1 large daikon, peeled and
    roughly chopped
1 tablespoon salt
1 tablespoon fish sauce
200g rock sugar, crushed
10 star anise
1 small cinnamon stick
5g cloves
10g coriander seeds
10g cardamom pods

Pork Stock

Canh Heo

Fill a stockpot with 4 litres of water and place over a high heat. Bring to the boil, then add the pork bones, trotters and ribs. Make sure that the water level is at least 2.5cm above the pork and boil for 3 minutes.

Take the pan off the heat, drain, clean the pot and rinse the pork under cold running water.

Return the parboiled pork back to the pot along with the remaining ingredients, and cover with 4 litres of water. Again, make sure that the water level is at least 2.5cm above the pork. Place over a high heat and bring the water to the boil over a high heat.

Skim off any impurities from the surface, cover with a lid, leaving a finger-width gap for the steam to escape. Lower the heat and simmer for 2 hours, skimming away any impurities during this time.

Take the pot off the heat and discard all of the large solids in the stock. Leave the stock to sit for 2 hours.

Strain the stock through a fine sieve into a large container, making sure to stop when you get close to the bottom of the pot as this will consist of mainly gritty residue from the flavouring ingredients.

Set the stock aside to cool completely, then store in the fridge for up to 3 days or freeze for up to 3 months.

Makes 2 litres

1kg pork bones
1kg pork trotters
1kg pork ribs
2 onions, peeled
1 large daikon, peeled and
    roughly chopped
2 tablespoons salt
200g rock sugar, crushed

Fish Stock

Canh Cá

Wash the fish bones thoroughly under cold running water.

Place the fish bones into a stockpot along with the onions, salt, fish sauce and crushed rock sugar, then pour in 4 litres of water. Set over a high heat and bring the water to the boil. Skim off any impurities from the surface, cover with a lid, leaving a finger-width gap for the steam to escape, and lower the heat. Simmer for 2 hours.

Check the stock after 1 hour and remove any further impurities from the surface.

Remove the pot from the heat, take out the large ingredients and skim off any impurities floating on the surface. Set aside to settle for 2 hours.

Strain the stock through a fine sieve into a large container, making sure to stop when you get close to the bottom of the pot as this will consist of mainly gritty residue from the flavouring ingredients.

Leave to cool fully on the side and then store in the fridge for up to 3 days or freeze for up to 3 months.

Makes 2 litres

3kg white fish bones
2 onions, peeled
1 tablespoon salt
1 tablespoon fish sauce
150g rock sugar, crushed

Vegetable Stock

Canh Chay

Put all the ingredients into a stockpot and pour in 4 litres of water. Set over a high heat and bring the water to the boil. Skim off any impurities from the surface, cover with a lid, leaving a finger-width gap for the steam to escape, and lower the heat. Simmer for 2 hours, then take the stock off the heat.

Take the large ingredients out of the stock and skim away any impurities floating on the surface of the stock. Set aside to settle for 2 hours.

Strain the stock through a fine sieve into a large container, making sure to stop when you get close to the bottom of the pot as this will consist of mainly gritty residue from the flavouring ingredients.

Set the stock aside to cool completely, then store in the fridge for up to 3 days or freeze for up to 3 months.

Makes 2 litres

2 onions, peeled
1 large swede, peeled and
  roughly chopped
1 large daikon, peeled and
  roughly chopped
2 celeriac, peeled and roughly
  chopped
6 large carrots, peeled
2 tablespoons salt
150g rock sugar, crushed

Home
Comforts

Home Comforts

True home-cooked Vietnamese comfort food is what I miss from my childhood. I miss seeing and hearing the physical signs of people enjoying the food without any words needed. I've always been a huge believer in interacting with food and I don't mean just the cooking of it. In general, family meals are great fun because they're relaxed, comfortable and perhaps even a little rude to the Western culture. There will always be the noise of loud slurping, chewing with your mouth wide open hoping to squeeze in the biggest portion possible and of course loud talking and lots of laughter. Many dishes rely on you using your hands to roll herbs or tear a pancake. There is the constant reaching of arms and leaning across to share plates, never accompanied by an 'excuse me' because it is just understood that it is a must. It took me a long while to understand the differences in culture and etiquette when I first moved to London and to this day I find it intriguing that some things are perfectly normal in one that are frowned upon in the other.

I naturally crave Vietnamese food; it's in my blood. However, oddly I think that I finally felt like London was my home the day I enjoyed my first big mac! I had spent years refusing to eat McDonald's and could not understand why the other kids saw it as such a treat; it had always looked disgusting to me. (Sorry Ronald.) But the day I relented and joined my schoolmates under the golden arches was the first day I realised that I was becoming a Londoner.

The dishes in this chapter are scrumptious and finger-licking worthy. Vietnamese food is almost always cooked on the bone so as not to lose the sweetness and texture, but it is generally chopped into bite-sized pieces so you don't have to actually lick your fingers. I have always considered myself an expert at deboning ribs with my tongue and teeth, no hands needed. OK, so not the best party trick in school, but it does mean I can eat a lot of them and very fast!

The aroma of these dishes remind me of my school days here in the UK, when I would rush home so fast because hunger would always hit me hard at 3pm. Mum would whip up something quick like sticky ribs, a vegetable stir fry on the side and a healthy clear meaty soup to help wash it all down. So as soon as dad walked in the front door, dinner was ready — although dad would often prefer a little rest from the long drive home which didn't sit well with my rumbling tummy! My patience has never been very good, which is probably why I put so much effort in to learning as many dishes as possible from mum. This meant that I could have whatever I was craving, whenever I wanted it. It's amazing how far you can come just by being greedy and ever-hungry!

Not every dish mum has taught me can quite hit the spot though. For some reason, even to this day, the occasional dish I make will still not taste quite as good as hers. I call it a mother's love in her cooking… They tend to have that one last extra teaspoon of something they 'forgot' to tell us about! My mum knows that at just one phone call, all three of her kids would run home if she mentioned thịt khô trứng was on the menu! It's an Asian mummy's power over her children.

For a Vietnamese mother, it is not normal to express her love with words; it's all done through the food on the table and my belly is very ok with that!

Coconut Braised Pork and Egg

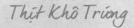

To my mind this is the ultimate home comfort food. It never fails to bring back fond memories of large family meals, generally for a special occasion like Tết (New Year) or a wedding celebration as pork was considered a luxury, so symbolises wealth and fortune.

This is a beautiful and simple dish that showcases the key technique in Vietnamese cooking of slow braising in coconut water. Sweet, salty and spicy, it is best accompanied with sour and bitter pickles and is perfectly balanced by serving with fluffy jasmine rice.

Slow cooked in the natural sweetness of coconut water, the pork is so juicy and tender that every bite melts in your mouth. Perhaps it is because we had this dish so rarely that even to this day I savour every mouthful like it's my last.

Put all of the pork along with the ingredients for the marinade in a bowl. Mix together well and leave in the fridge overnight to marinate.

Heat the oil in a large saucepan over a high heat until it reaches 190°C. An easy way to tell when the oil is ready is to place a wooden chopstick into it – when bubbles form on the surface of the oil it is ready.

Add the pork along with its marinade and the caramel sauce. Toss the pork continually for about 4 minutes, until the caramel sauce has fully and evenly coated all of the pork. It is crucial to keep stirring the pork as it only takes a couple of seconds for it to go from golden to burnt.

Now add the coconut water and 300ml of water, and bring to the boil. Skim off any impurities and marinade ingredients that float to the surface. The sauce needs to be clear and not cloudy. Turn down the heat and simmer for 2 hours.

Add the fish sauce, the whole peeled hard-boiled eggs and the chillies, and continue to simmer for a further hour.

Remove the pan from the heat and serve with mustard cabbage pickle and a generous portion of rice. A bowl of fish sauce with some sliced red chillies in would also make a good accompaniment.

Serves 5–6

500g pork belly, cut into 5cm dice
500g pork leg, cut into 5cm dice
3 tablespoons vegetable oil
2 teaspoons Caramel Sauce (page 27)
1 litre coconut water
3 tablespoons fish sauce
8 hard-boiled eggs, peeled
3 red chillies
Pickled Mustard Cabbage (page 23), to serve

For the marinade
2 bird's eye chillies, crushed
8 Asian shallots, crushed
8 garlic cloves, crushed
juice of 1 lime
1 tablespoon granulated sugar
1 teaspoon salt

Caramelised Coconut Catfish

Cá Ba Sa Kho Tộ

A humble dish, but one that brings an explosion of flavour and warmth to any mealtime. If you want to go really 'farm' on this dish then you can add lots of extra fish sauce. This makes it much saltier than the classic recipe but is done so often in rural areas of Vietnam that there is a name for the technique, khô quẹt. This basically translates as a caramelisation so thick that you have to scrape the clay pot clean.

Traditionally this dish is cooked using a clay pot, however a saucepan will work just fine. The clay pot just allows more heat to be retained, speeding up the caramelising process and staying hot for longer on the dining table … not a problem I've ever needed solving!

A sweet and sour prawn soup (page 62) is the perfect partner for this, so if you would like an authentic Vietnamese home-style meal try cooking both together.

Put the fish and all the ingredients for the marinade in a bowl, and mix together well. Leave in the fridge for at least 3 hours, or ideally overnight. Take the fish out of the fridge 30 minutes before cooking to allow it to come to room temperature.

Heat the oil in a saucepan over a medium heat until it reaches 160°C. An easy way to tell when the oil is ready is to place a wooden chopstick into it – when bubbles form on the surface of the oil it is ready. Add in the green peppercorns and the whole chilli, then sauté for 1 minute.

Remove the fish from the marinade and add to the pan. Set the remaining marinade aside for later. Fry the fish for 2 minutes, then turn over and fry the other side for a further 2 minutes. Pour in the coconut water and the reserved marinade. Turn the heat up to high and cook for a further 3–4 minutes. The liquid will reduce down and the fish should brown and caramelise. At this point, turn the heat off.

Transfer the fish to a serving plate and garnish with the chilli, spring onion curls and a sprinkle of crushed black peppercorns.

This dish is best served with a handful of herbs and steamed jasmine rice to offset the saltiness of the caramelised fish. A simple dipping sauce of fish sauce and sliced red chillies served on the side would also be perfect.

Serves 4

500g basa catfish or cod fillets
2 tablespoons vegetable oil
100g green peppercorns
1 bird's eye chilli
200ml coconut water

For the marinade

1 teaspoon finely diced garlic
3 teaspoons finely diced Asian
  shallots
2 tablespoons soft brown sugar
3 tablespoons fish sauce
3 teaspoons sesame oil
1 teaspoon Caramel Sauce
  (page 27)

To serve

1 bird's eye chilli, thinly sliced
  diagonally
6 spring onions, sliced into thin
  strips and soaked in cold water
  for 20 minutes until curled
½ teaspoon crushed black
  peppercorns
large handful of herbs, such as
  Thai basil or mint

Ginger Chicken

Gà Kho Gừng

'Zesty with a little heat' is a perfect description for this dish! It is fragrant from the moment the ginger sizzles in the pan, almost overpoweringly so. As a child, I was often told to 'eat up all your ginger, it will keep your body warm and scare off the flu'; true or not (obviously not) I grew up eating every single piece of ginger in this dish in the hope that it would make me invincible. What it definitely did was make me absolutely love that kick of mild spice and warmth that ginger gives you!

Cut the chicken legs and thighs into rough 5cm chunks using a sharp cleaver or knife (if you prefer, ask your butcher to do this). Be careful to make the cuts as clean as possible – you don't want shards of bone in your dish. Soak the chicken pieces in plenty of cold water, adding the salt. Leave to soak for 2 minutes then gently rub the chicken to complete the cleaning. Drain the chicken pieces. Pat dry with paper towels.

Put the chicken pieces and all of the marinade ingredients into a large bowl. Mix well and rub the marinade all over the chicken. Cover with clingfilm and place in the fridge to marinate for a minimum of 3 hours, or ideally overnight.

Heat the oil in a large frying pan over a medium heat until it reaches 160°C. An easy way to tell when the oil is ready is to place a wooden chopstick into it – when bubbles form on the surface of the oil it is ready. Put the chicken, along with its marinade, into the pan and gently stir-fry for 5 minutes until the chicken starts to brown.

Add the caramel sauce and continue to stir-fry for a further minute. Make sure to keep a close eye on the chicken at this point as the sugar can burn very easily.

Pour in the coconut water and lower the heat. Simmer for 10 minutes, stirring occasionally. Add the ginger, chillies, peppercorns and shallots, and continue to cook for a further 5 minutes, stirring occasionally. At this stage, the liquid will have reduced to a thick and sticky consistency and the chicken will be a beautiful golden brown colour.

I love this served with steamed jasmine rice.

Serves 4–5 as part of a meal of many sharing dishes

350g chicken legs
350g chicken thighs
1 tablespoon salt
2 tablespoons vegetable oil
1 teaspoon Caramel Sauce (page 27)
300ml coconut water
300g ginger, cut into fine matchsticks
2 bird's eye chillies, sliced diagonally
1 teaspoon crushed black peppercorns
1 tablespoon Crispy Fried Shallots (page 25)

For the marinade
200g Asian shallots, finely diced
1 tablespoons soy sauce
2 tablespoons garlic, finely diced
2 tablespoons granulated sugar
1 teaspoon salt
1 tablespoon fish sauce
2 teaspoons crushed black peppercorns
3 tablespoons sesame oil

Baked Squid Stuffed with Pork

Mực Nướng Nhồi Thịt

This dish is great as a sharing starter, or with some jasmine rice and fish dipping sauce as a main course. Either way, it's really delicious and sure to impress your dinner guests!

First prepare the squid. Spread one of the squid out and reach up inside to remove all the internal organs including the pen, which looks like a plastic feather, and throw all the internal organs away.

Cut the tentacles away from the body just below the eyes, clean and reserve. Give the squid a good squeeze at the base so that the beak pops out and then remove the beak. Cut or pull the purple skin from the squid to leave just the white meat.

Cut the fins from the squid and discard. (It's worth noting that they are not only edible but also delicious, so try trimming the hard edge and throwing them in a stir-fry to add a lovely chewy seafood texture.)

Now thoroughly rinse the squid both inside and out to ensure you have all the internals removed along with any sand or grit that may be in there. Repeat the process for the remaining squid and you're ready to start cooking!

Boil 1 litre of water and pour into a large bowl. Soak the glass noodles for 20 minutes, then drain, dry and cut into pieces roughly 2 inches long. Repeat the process for the dried black fungus with another litre of water.

In a large mixing bowl, combine the noodles and mushroom and all of the stuffing mixture ingredients and mix together well. Stuff the squid with the pork mixture, making sure to pack it in firmly.

Preheat the oven to 180°C/160°C Fan/Gas Mark 4.

Heat the vegetable oil to a high heat in a frying pan; the oil is hot enough when bubbles appear around the end of a chopstick when dipped in. Fry the squid for 2–3 minutes, moving and turning them continuously to ensure an even colour.

Transfer the squid to a baking tray and bake in the oven for 10 minutes. Once cooked, take the squid out and leave to rest for a further 5 minutes.

Now plate up the squid and tentacles and drizzle over the chilli and lemongrass marinade for that final kick!

Serves 4–6

6 whole baby squid, 50–60g each
2 tablespoons vegetable oil
2 tablespoon Chilli and
    Lemongrass Marinade
    (page 21)

For the pork stuffing
25g dried glass noodles
10g dried black fungus
    mushroom
125g minced pork
50g carrots, very finely sliced
    or julienned
15g white cabbage, thinly sliced
25g water chestnuts, tinned,
    drained and diced
1 large spring onion, finely
    chopped
½ tablespoons granulated sugar
¼ tablespoon salt
½ teaspoon fish sauce
½ tablespoon sesame oil
½ tablespoons crushed black
    peppercorn
1 egg white, whisked

Grilled Soy-glazed Aubergine

Cà Tím Nướng Nước Tương Mỡ Hành

Soft, sweet and savoury, this delicately flavoured vegetable dish is super easy to make and the perfect accompaniment to almost anything! Every time I make this, I ask myself why I don't make it more often. It's definitely near the top of my 'forgotten-awesome-dish-list'! It's so easy to forget that the simplest recipes often keep the natural flavours of the ingredients the best. People often eat aubergine without the skin, but for me it is the best part so I urge you to keep the skin on as it's not only delicious, with a wonderful crispy texture, but it's full of healthy antioxidants too.

Preheat the oven to 200°C/Fan 180°C/Gas Mark 6.

Place the aubergines in a roasting tray and rub with the oil. Using a fork, poke lots of holes evenly around the aubergines. (This will help reduce the cooking time.) Roast in the oven for 25–30 minutes, or until soft and collapsing.

Meanwhile, make the glaze. In a small saucepan, add the sesame oil and annatto seed oil. When hot, add the garlic and chillies, and fry for 15 seconds. Add in the coconut water, soy sauce, sugar and honey, and bring to the boil. Lastly, add the spring onions and turn the heat off immediately. You only want to slightly cook the spring onions, retaining their vibrant green colour.

When the aubergines are done, remove from the oven and leave to cool for 2 minutes. If you prefer you can peel the skins off, although personally I love them left on.

To serve, slice open the aubergines by making a shallow cut from the stem to the base and then gently pulling the sides apart. Drizzle the soy glaze over the top and sprinkle with the crispy fired shallots and crushed black peppercorns to finish.

This is a perfect side dish to accompany rice and other Vietnamese dishes as part of a traditional Vietnamese family meal.

Serves 2

2 aubergines
2 teaspoons vegetable oil

For the soy glaze
3 tablespoons sesame oil
1 tablespoon Annatto Seed Oil (page 22)
2 teaspoons finely diced garlic
2 teaspoons finely diced red chillies
4 tablespoons coconut water
4 tablespoons soy sauce
2 tablespoons granulated sugar
1 tablespoon honey
6 tablespoons finely chopped spring onions

To serve
2 teaspoons Crispy Fried Shallots (page 25)
1 teaspoon crushed black peppercorns

Baked Sea Bass with Lemongrass, Chilli and Ginger

Cá Chẽm Nướng Sả Ớt Và Gừng

A real show stopper of a dish, this is ideal for hosting a dinner with friends or at weekend family gatherings. When cooked correctly, the combination of the crispy skin contrasting with the moist and flaky lemongrass- and ginger-infused meat is unbeatable!

Preheat the oven to 180°C/140°C Fan/Gas Mark 4.

Place the fish on a chopping board. Using a sharp knife, score across the fish and through the skin 4–5 times on each side. Then, use the knife to open up the belly as far back to the spine as you can without cutting through.

Insert the lemongrass stalks, garlic, chilli, ginger and lime slices into the belly. Use a kitchen string to tie the fish, securing the ingredients within the belly. Alternatively, use a toothpick to close the opening.

Place in a roasting dish and rub the entire exterior of the fish with sesame oil. Sprinkle the fish sauce over the fish skin. This will add flavour and help to crisp up the skin when cooked. Bake in the oven for 20 minutes, until the fish appears opaque and can easily be flaked.

As a complete Vietnamese meal, this could be served either as summer rolls – with pieces of fish flaked and wrapped together with herbs in rice paper and fish dipping sauce (page 28) – or with jasmine rice alongside a vegan soy dipping sauce (page 30).

Serves 1, or 4 as part of a meal of many sharing dishes

1 sea bass, gutted and descaled (about 400g)
2 lemongrass stalks, halved
3 garlic cloves, crushed
1 red chilli, crushed and halved
15cm piece ginger, sliced
3 lime slices
2 tablespoons sesame oil
1 teaspoon fish sauce

Honey and Coconut Caramelised Chicken Thighs

Thịt Gà Khìa Nước Dừa Mật Ong

On the Mekong Delta, coconuts are everywhere! They are essentially a free ingredient: as with so many growing naturally, they work out cheaper to buy than water! This goes some way to explaining why so many dishes from the region have coconuts as a key ingredient. For this recipe, the juice of the young coconut is used to tenderise the chicken whilst adding sweetness during the caramelisation. Mum often used to pack the leftovers for our school lunches and I would always get lots of envious looks from the other kids with their Dairylee sandwiches. Swapsies? No thanks!

In a mixing bowl, combine the chicken thighs and all of the ingredients for the marinade. Rub the ingredients into each thigh, and then leave to marinate for 1 hour in the fridge.

In a frying pan, over a medium heat, add the vegetable oil. Lay one chicken thigh, skin-side down, and fry for 2–3 minutes, depending on size, until the skin is golden but without completely cooking the chicken. Take out and set aside to cool down, repeating the process for the remaining chicken thighs individually.

Remove any burnt bits of marinade, and add all 12 chicken thighs back into the pan, skin-side facing up. Add the onion, coconut water and any excess marinade left in the bowl, then cover the pan with a lid and cook over a low heat for 25 minutes. This should cook the chicken through slowly, tenderising the meat.

When the 25 minutes is up, take the lid off and increase the heat to high. Drizzle the honey on top of the chicken, making sure you do not at any point take your eyes off the pan. You will see caramelisation take place very quickly so keep turning the thighs over, allowing them to become evenly golden. Do this for 2–3 minutes, until the liquid becomes syrupy and the chicken perfectly golden.

Not necessary, but a quick blast under the grill for 2 minutes will give a wonderful crispy skin – a bonus for sure.

Serve with fish sauce as a starter, or with jasmine rice as a main. Both are absolutely delicious.

Serves 4

12 chicken thighs, on the bone
4 tablespoons vegetable oil
2 large onions, sliced into 2cm thick pieces
750ml coconut water, strain any pulp
3 tablespoons honey
fish sauce, to serve

For the marinade
2 tablespoons granulated sugar
2 teaspoons salt
1 tablespoon fish sauce
10 spring onions, white part only, finely chopped
2–3 red chillies, finely chopped
10 garlic cloves, finely chopped
3 tablespoons sesame oil

Vietnamese Garlic Broccoli Stir-fry

Rau Cải Làn Xào Tỏi Và Sả Tế

This simple recipe is perfect as a side or a large portion to share. Get your timings right and you'll keep all the goodness locked in! The broccoli should be bright in colour, glistening on the plate and joyfully crunchy on the bite.

Bring 1 litre of water to the boil, and blanch the broccoli stems for 20 seconds then immediately submerge into a large bowl of cold water. Leave for 30 seconds, then take out and drain.

Heat the sesame oil to a medium heat in a small frying pan. An easy way to tell when the oil is ready is to place a wooden chopstick into it – when bubbles form on the surface of the oil it is ready. Add the crushed garlic, keeping it moving around the pan for approximately 10 seconds until the colour begins to change to a light brown.

Add the broccoli, soy sauce and sugar and toss for 1 minute making sure that the broccoli is coated evenly in the sauce.

Remove the broccoli stems from the heat immediately, ensuring it remains al dente, and plate.

Now drizzle over the chilli and lemongrass marinade and it's ready to serve!

Serves 2–3

300g Asian broccoli, washed and
  dried
3 tablespoons sesame oil
6 garlic cloves, crushed
2 teaspoons soy sauce
1 teaspoon granulated sugar
1 tablespoon Chilli and
  Lemongrass Marinade
  (page 21)

Sweet and Sour Prawn Soup

Canh Chua Tôm

This is a traditional Vietnamese dish that might be a little sharper than Western palates are used to. I've suggested half a pineapple here but if you want true authenticity then use a whole one. It's primarily for flavouring — we don't necessarily eat all of it. If you have this dish in Vietnam then you'd find elephant ear stems included, but they are hard to find in the UK so it can be optional.

I use huge jumbo prawns (think extra, extra large), but if you can't find these then just make sure you have one kilogram of the prawns you choose.

Make the dipping sauce by combining the ingredients in a small bowl. Set aside.

In a saucepan, bring 300ml of water to the boil over a high heat. Add the tamarind pulp, and break it down with a pestle until fully dissolved. The pips and some residue will remain. Strain the tamarind water through a sieve into a bowl using a spoon to press down as much liquid as possible. Discard the solids. Rinse the saucepan and pour the tamarind water back into the pan.

Add the fish stock and bring to the boil. Stir in the pineapple, sugar and fish sauce, and cook for 1 minute. Add the okra, tomatoes and prawns, reduce the heat to medium, and continue to cook for 3 minutes.

Now add the elephant's ear and bean sprouts, and bring back up to the boil.

Taste the soup at this stage. This is where you can adjust the sweetness and saltiness to your taste. The beauty of this dish is that it has many elements of taste working together, so tweaking one or the other to your preference is exactly the point.

Now add the fresh herbs and the chilli and immediately turn off the heat.

Ladle the soup into a large serving bowl and sprinkle with the crispy garlic and shallots. Serve with rice, banana blossom (if you are using) and the dipping sauce. It's also delicious served with the caramelised coconut catfish (page 43).

Serves 4

300g tamarind pulp
1.2 litres Fish Stock (page 35)
½–1 ripe pineapple, peeled and sliced into 1 x 4cm long pieces
3 tablespoons granulated sugar
2 tablespoons fish sauce
10 okra, halved
12 cherry tomatoes
4 jumbo king prawns, 1kg total, peeled and deveined and heads left on
2 stems elephant ear plant (optional), sliced diagonally
150g bean sprouts
small handful of rice paddy herb, finely chopped
small handful of sawtooth coriander, finely chopped
small handful of Thai basil, finely chopped
2 bird's eye chillies, thinly sliced

For the dipping sauce
20ml fish sauce
3 bird's eye chillies, thinly sliced diagonally

To serve
1 tablespoon Crispy Garlic (page 26)
1 tablespoon Crispy Fried Shallots (page 25)
banana blossom (optional)

Chicken Rice Porridge

Cháo Gà

The definitive Vietnamese home comfort food, cháo gà is a breakfast dish that is still eaten every day in rural Vietnam. However, to most Vietnamese people, it is known as the food you're given when you're ill. As soon as the first sniffle of a cold hits, Viet mums are rushing to the kitchen to prepare a big bowl of cháo gà.

Elsewhere in Vietnam, it might be served with Chinese doughnuts to be dunked into the porridge as a side, offering a tasty contrasting chewy texture. But, where I am from on the Mekong Delta, it always comes with a huge cabbage side salad and a ginger dipping sauce. That ginger and chilli heat is guaranteed to cure any man flu.

Make the salad by combining the cabbage, red onions, carrots and both mints in a bowl. Add the fish sauce and lime salad dressing and sprinkle the shallots and peanuts, if using, on top. Place in the fridge until ready to serve.

In a bowl, combine both rices and add enough water to cover by 5cm. Leave for 1 hour to soak, then drain.

In a stockpot, bring 2 litres of water to the boil over a high heat. Add the chicken and 1 teaspoon of salt, and allow to boil for 10 minutes. Skim off any impurities that rise to the surface, reduce to a medium heat and simmer for a further 45 minutes.

Take the chicken out of the pot and transfer to an ice bath for 5 minutes – this stops the chicken from cooking any further. Leave to rest.

Add the drained rice, the onions and the crushed ginger to the pot. Lower the heat and simmer for a further 1 hour, adding a little more water as needed.

The contents of the pot should now resemble porridge, with a thick consistency and lovely texture. Season with the fish sauce, salt and sugar and bring the heat up to boiling point once more. Keep stirring constantly for the next 2 minutes, making sure everything is mixed well. This is the one dish that you want to be mushy.

Chop the chicken into pieces around 2cm wide and 4cm long, and place on a plate. Add the crispy fried shallots, ginger slices and fish sauce, or keep this on the side for dipping; it's completely up to you! I like the sauce to soak into the meat.

To serve, remove the whole onions and dish the porridge up into a bowl. You can either serve all the separate elements at the table for everyone to help themselves from, or add the chicken to the porridge and garnish with spring onions, ginger, coriander and crispy fried shallots. Serve alongside the cabbage salad and the fiery gingery fish sauce and it's ready to eat.

Serves 4–5

250g glutinous rice
250g jasmine rice
1 whole corn-fed chicken, approx 1.5kg
2 onions, peeled
100g ginger, cut into 2cm thick slices, then crushed
1 tablespoon fish sauce
2 teaspoons granulated sugar
salt

For the cabbage salad
250g white cabbage, shredded
250g purple cabbage, shredded
2 red onions, finely sliced
3 carrots, cut into fine matchsticks
20g Vietnamese mint, finely chopped
20g mint, finely chopped
4 tablespoons Fish Sauce and Lime Salad Dressing (page 28)
1 tablespoon Crispy Fried Shallots (page 25)
1 tablespoon Roasted Peanuts (page 26), optional

To serve
6 spring onions, finely sliced
10g ginger, cut into fine matchsticks
20g coriander, finely chopped
1 tablespoon Crispy Fried Shallots (page 25)
Ginger Fish Sauce (page 29)

Pork and Egg Terrine

Chả Trứng Hấp

Traditionally served as a side with broken rice, this is just as delicious when served with jasmine rice as part of a family meal. I never really know how to describe this when I get asked, as it's an amalgamation of an omelette, meatloaf and terrine. However, all you really need to know is that it is absolutely scrumptious!

Make the egg mixture first by whipping the egg yolks, shallots and spring onions in a small bowl. Set aside for later.

In a large bowl, combine all the ingredients for the meat mixture and knead well. The mince needs to be fully broken up so make sure to do this thoroughly. Put the mixture in a large casserole dish or 23cm cake tin.

If you have a steamer then you'll know exactly how to set it up. Alternatively, fill a large saucepan halfway up with water and use a small cooking tripod (available in all kitchen stores) to prop the dish up (or place a small bowl upside down in the saucepan and sit the dish on top). It is essential that the dish does not touch the water and that the saucepan is deep enough that a lid can be placed on top leaving plenty of space above the dish for the terrine to steam. Place the lid on and steam for 20 minutes. Pour the egg yolk mixture over the top and continue to steam for a further 10 minutes until the egg is set.

Traditionally, this terrine is served as part of a lunch dish with broken rice grains, a dipping sauce and caramelised pork chops, but I love to serve it as a baguette filling or simple side or starter. Either way, it's deliciously satisfying.

Serves 8–10

For the egg mixture
4 duck egg yolks, lightly beaten
5 Asian shallots, thinly sliced
3 spring onions, thinly sliced on the diagonal

For the meat mixture
500g pork mince
100g dried vermicelli glass noodles, soaked in warm water for 30 minutes, drained and cut into 4cm strips
100g wood ear mushrooms, soaked in warm water for 30 minutes, drained then finely diced
240g tinned crabmeat, drained
2 tablespoons fish sauce
1 tablespoon granulated sugar
½ teaspoon salt
1 tablespoon crushed black peppercorns
3 tablespoons vegetable oil
6 spring onions, finely chopped
1 onion, finely diced
1 tablespoon finely diced garlic
4 duck eggs, lightly beaten
4 duck egg whites, lightly beaten

To serve (optional)
spring onions, thinly sliced
Crispy Fried Shallots (page 25)
peppercorns
Vietnamese mint

Lemongrass Honey Pork

Thịt Heo Nướng Sả Và Mật Ong

The honey gives a smooth sweetness that takes this pork to another level of happiness for your belly.

Put all the marinade ingredients into a food processor and blitz for 15 seconds. This step is optional. You can be more traditional and simply combine the diced and liquid ingredients, perhaps grinding the peppercorns in a mortar and pestle first. There is something homely and comforting about the gritty bits and their magical surges of flavour that the traditional method retains. However, blitzing will give a smoother texture and the ingredients will be more evenly spread throughout the marinade.

Add the pork and marinade to a bowl. Use clean hands to massage and rub the marinade into the pork. Cover the bowl with clingfilm and place in the fridge to marinate for at least 3 hours, or ideally overnight.

Take the pork out of the fridge 30–45 minutes before cooking to give it a chance to come up to room temperature.

Preheat the oven to 160°C/140°C Fan/Gas Mark 3.

Arrange the pork pieces on a baking tray, spreading over some of the marinade and leaving the rest aside for later. Cook for 10 minutes, turning the pork pieces after 5 minutes.

Increase the oven temperature to 180°C/160°C Fan/Gas Mark 4. Spread the reserved marinade over the pork and cook for a further 20 minutes.

Take the pork out of the oven and allow 5–10 minutes for it to rest.

This is best served with rice, salad vegetables or a simple stir-fry of your choice. It's also wonderful for lunch served with a crusty baguette.

Serves 4

1kg boneless pork loin, portioned into 4

For the marinade

4 tablespoons onions, finely diced
3 tablespoons honey
1 tablespoon soft brown sugar
2 teaspoons black peppercorns
½ teaspoon salt
1 tablespoon fish sauce
2 tablespoons soy sauce
4 stems lemongrass, finely diced
2 tablespoons garlic, finely diced
6 tablespoons sesame oil

Caramelised Prawns and Pork Belly

Tôm Rang Thịt Ba Chỉ

Everyone loves prawns and who can say no to belly pork? Add to that the beautiful sweetness and saltiness of the caramelisation and you have a rural Vietnamese classic that will warm your belly on even the coldest of days. Like all farm dishes this is simple to make with no fancy ingredients, but I warn you … prepare to waddle away from the table. It's so moreish it's hard to stop!

In a bowl, combine the marinade ingredients, then add half of the marinade mixture to the prawns. Mix together well and leave to marinate for 3 hours.

In a separate bowl, combine the remaining marinade with the pork belly. Mix together well and leave to marinate for 3 hours.

Heat the oil in a saucepan over a medium heat. Add the garlic and lemongrass and fry briefly, until golden. Next, add the pork belly (and its marinade) and chillies, tossing for 3 minutes, then stir in the prawns (and their marinade). Continue to stir-fry for a further 3 minutes, add the spring onions and cook for another minute – the pork and prawns should be beautifully caramelised so turn up the heat if necessary.

This dish is best served alongside rice and other dishes such as a soup or a vegetable stir-fry.

Serves 4 as part of a meal of many sharing dishes

300g raw prawns, heads on and
   tails trimmed (see Salt and
   Pepper King Prawns, page 141)
300g pork belly, cut into
   2mm dice
3 tablespoons vegetable oil
2 tablespoons finely diced garlic
6 tablespoons finely diced
   lemongrass stalks
2 bird's eye chillies
6 stems spring onions

For the marinade
2 tablespoons soft brown sugar
2 tablespoons fish sauce
2 tablespoons soy sauce
1½–2 tablespoons black
   peppercorns, crushed
2 tablespoons vegetable oil
10 Asian shallots, finely diced

Pork-stuffed Bitter Melon

Khổ Qua Nhồi Thịt Heo

This dish is not for everybody's taste buds, but for me the bitter, salty, sweet and spicy flavours all exploding together is an amazing experience on the palate and one that I simply couldn't leave out of the book. Whilst this is a classic dish that is universally liked in Vietnam, it has proven to be the Vietnamese 'Marmite' when I've shared it with friends in London. Will you be 'team love it' or 'team hate it'? The only thing I can say for certain is you won't be sitting on the fence.

Put all of the ingredients for the stuffing in a large bowl and mix well, making sure to break up all of the mince. Cover with clingfilm and place in the fridge for a minimum of 3 hours, or ideally overnight.

Using a sharp knife, make a cut in one of the bitter melons down its length. Prise out the white pips. Scoop the filling mix into the cavity of the bitter melon, making sure it's not too tightly packed as the meat will expand when cooked. Repeat with the remaining melons.

In a large saucepan, bring 3 litres of water to the boil over a high heat and drop in the melons. Allow to boil for 5 minutes, then skim off any impurities that float to the surface.

Lower the heat to medium and simmer for 25 minutes, until just firm. Add the fish sauce, sugar and salt to the pan and continue to simmer for a further 5 minutes. At this point, the melons should be soft enough to pierce with a fork yet not fall apart.

In a small bowl, combine the fish sauce and chillies to make a dipping sauce.

Serve the stuffed bitter melons garnished with the spring onions, coriander (if using) and a pinch of crushed black peppercorns. Ladle the broth between serving bowls and serve on the side alongside some jasmine rice and the dipping sauce for dunking the melons into.

Serves 6

6 bitter melons (approx 1kg)
1 teaspoon fish sauce
1 tablespoon granulated sugar
1 teaspoon salt

For the stuffing

300g minced pork
100g dried glass noodles, soaked for 30 minutes in warm water, drained and cut into 4cm lengths
50g dried black fungus, soaked for 30 minutes in warm water, drained and finely chopped
6 spring onions, finely chopped
1 tablespoon granulated sugar
1 teaspoon salt
1 teaspoon fish sauce
1 tablespoon sesame oil

For the dipping sauce

100ml fish sauce
2 bird's eye chillies, thinly sliced diagonally

To serve

3 spring onions, finely chopped
20g coriander (optional)
crushed black peppercorns

Caramelised Honey and Coconut Water Pork Chops

Thịt Heo Khìa Nước Dừa Và Mật Ong

Traditionally this dish would be served alongside the pork and egg terrine (page 67) as part of a meal called cơm tấm, which translates as broken rice. The origin of this paring is from rural Vietnam where the rice farmers would be left with the often-unsellable, broken rice for their family's dinner. They would eat this with these beautifully caramelised pork chops. Not wanting to waste food, the offcuts of the pork would then be used to make mince and this in turn would be made into the pork and egg terrine, then served together with a salad topped with bì, shredded pork skin. Generations later they are still often eaten together, but all stand alone as amazing dishes in their own right.

In a bowl, combine the pork chops and all the ingredients for the marinade. Rub the marinade into each pork chop evenly, then leave for at least 3 hours to marinate in the fridge. If you have time, marinating them overnight will create even better results.

Heat 4 tablespoons of vegetable oil in a frying pan over a medium heat until it reaches 160°C. An easy way to tell when the oil is ready is to place a wooden chopstick into it – when bubbles form on the surface of the oil it is ready.

Add the pork chops (reserving any marinade left behind) and fry for 90 seconds on each side until golden but not completely cooked through. Now add the coconut water and the reserved marinade. Partially cover the pan with the lid, and cook for a further 20 minutes.

Take off the lid, increase the heat to high and pour the honey over the pork chops. You will see the caramelisation take place very quickly, so keep turning the chops over to coat them evenly in the honey. Do not take your eyes off the pan during this process, as the chops will burn quicker than you expect. Cook for 3–5 minutes (depending on your pan size), until the liquid thickens to a syrupy consistency and the pork chops are perfectly golden.

You can either slice the chops or serve them whole. Whichever you decide, add the pork to your plates along with a portion of fluffy jasmine rice. Garnish with the spring onions, and mint leaves and coriander if using. A side salad of your choice drizzled with fish sauce and sprinkled with crispy fried shallots would also go down a treat.

Serves 4

4 t-bone pork chops, 200g each
4 tablespoons vegetable oil
300ml coconut water
3 tablespoons honey

For the marinade

2 tablespoons granulated sugar
1 teaspoon salt
1 tablespoon fish sauce
3 tablespoons sesame oil
10 spring onions, white parts only, crushed and finely chopped
2–3 red chillies, crushed and finely chopped
10 garlic cloves, finely chopped

To serve

spring onions, finely sliced
100g mint leaves, optional
100g coriander, optional

Coconut Beef Stew

Bò Kho

When it's cold outside and all you want to do is wrap up indoors, this is the perfect dish to warm you up. The aroma around the house just while cooking this dish is enough to keep me warm in winter. Savoury, salty with the subtle sweetness of coconut, this stew is a classic Vietnamese dish that can be served a number of ways depending on the time of day you eat it. At breakfast you might have bò kho with a crusty baguette, for lunch you could ladle it over a big bowl of rice noodles and fresh herbs, and for dinner it would be accompanied by steamed rice. Make your choice, or, like me, cook a pot big enough to last for all three meals.

In the south of Vietnam, much like pho, this is traditionally a breakfast favourite. While that may seem very strange to Westerners, there is a logic to getting something hearty in your belly before setting off for a long day working in the rice fields.

One thing I need to mention is you need patience for this recipe. If you are anything like me, you may be tempted to open the oven door and check on the stew every few minutes to see if it's ready. Checking will not speed up the cooking time — if anything it will slow it down a little — no matter how irresistible the smell every time the oven door is opened. Wait.

First prepare the marinade. In a dry frying pan, toast the spices for 4–5 minutes over a medium heat. You should smell the aromatic flavours as the spices toast. Tip into a spice grinder, and blitz for 15–20 seconds, until you have a fine powder.

Put the beef brisket, beef shin and oxtail into a large bowl, and add the ground spices and remaining ingredients for the marinade. Mix together well and leave in the fridge for a minimum of 3 hours but overnight if you can.

Preheat the oven to 150°C/130°C Fan/Gas Mark 2.

Heat the annatto seed oil in a large casserole pan over a high heat and add the beef along with all of its marinade. It is best to do this in batches to prevent overcrowding the pan. Fry the beef, stirring only occasionally to brown, for 4 minutes. Add the sundried tomato paste, rice wine, coconut water, bay leaves and crushed lemongrass. Turn up the heat to high, bring to the boil and simmer gently for 10 minutes. Cover the pan with a lid and place in the oven for 2½ hours. Try to resist the urge to check on the stew…

Remove the casserole from the oven, add the carrots and return to the oven for a further 25 minutes. Add the onions, then cook for a further 5 minutes … and the wait is finally over.

Ladle the stew between serving bowls and garnish with the herbs and chillies. A squeeze of lime adds a wonderful zing to the savoury meaty juice. Serve with toasted baguette and a side of the salt, pepper and lime seasoning.

Serves 6

750g beef brisket, cut into 4cm dice
750g beef shin, cut into 4cm dice
200g oxtail, cut into pieces about 5cm thick
75ml Annatto Seed Oil (page 22)
180g sundried tomato paste
2 tablespoons rice wine
1 litre coconut water
4 bay leaves
4 lemongrass stalks, halved and bashed
300g baby carrots, or 4 large carrots, cut diagonally into 1cm thick slices
2 large onions, cut into wedges

For the marinade
10 star anise
5 dried red chillies
2 cinnamon sticks
3 cloves
1½ teaspoons black peppercorns
2 tablespoons finely diced Asian shallots
2 tablespoons finely diced garlic
2 tablespoons finely diced lemongrass stalks
2 tablespoons finely diced red chillies
2 tablespoons granulated sugar
2 tablespoons fish sauce

To serve
20g Thai basil leaves
20g coriander leaves
2 large spring onions, finely chopped
2 red chillies, finely chopped
2 limes, cut into wedges
6 crusty baguettes, toasted
Salt, Pepper and Lime Seasoning (page 27)

Sticky Ribs Caramelised in Coconut Water

Sườn Khìa Nước Dừa

These sticky ribs are delicious served with the carrot and daikon pickle on page 23 and a side salad.

Heat the oil in a large frying pan over a medium heat until it reaches 160°C. An easy way to tell when the oil is ready is to place a wooden chopstick into it – when bubbles form on the surface of the oil it is ready. Add the garlic, onion and chillies, and sauté for 1 minute until golden brown.

Add the ribs, the fish sauce and the caramel sauce or sugar. Stir continuously for 5 minutes to prevent the sugar from burning, and when the ribs appear caramelised, pour in the coconut water. Cover with the lid, lower the heat and simmer for 35–45 minutes. The longer you leave the ribs to cook, the more tender they will become.

Next, remove the lid, add the spring onions, and toss everything together. Turn the heat up to high and continue to toss the ribs for a further 5 minutes, or until the coconut water has almost completely reduced. Toss in the crushed black peppercorns.

Now you're ready to serve this dish accompanied by rice to offset the salty sweetness of the ribs. Garnish with the cucumber, lettuce, coriander and mint, if using. Have a bowl of the classic fish dipping sauce to hand, and you're good to go.

Serves 2

3 tablespoons vegetable oil
10 garlic cloves, crushed
2 tablespoons finely diced onion
5 red chillies, sliced lengthways
  into 2
1kg pork ribs, chopped into
  3cm pieces
3 tablespoons fish sauce
3 tablespoons Caramel Sauce
  (page 27) or soft brown sugar
300ml coconut water
6 tablespoons finely sliced
  spring onions
1 tablespoon crushed black
  peppercorns

To serve (optional)
1 cucumber, sliced 1cm thick
  on the diagonal
2 baby gem lettuces, leaves
  separated
100g coriander
100g mint
300ml Classic Fish Dipping
  Sauce (page 28)

Pho

When it comes to Vietnamese food, pho is the dish that truly represents the heart and soul of the country. Our national dish, traditionally eaten as breakfast, is now eaten worldwide at any time of the day or night. A humble dish, yet the delicate balance of spices and flavours helps to make it one that home cooks and professional chefs alike can be proud of.

'A secret not so secret'

As my mum would always tell me, it's all about the broth. Even the smallest detail can make the biggest difference to the final result of this beautiful dish. Here are my tips on how to make good pho:

The bones: Choose marrow-rich beef bones, such as knuckles or leg bones. Avoid neck bones.

Organic: Opting for organic produce and meat is entirely up to you, but I do recommend it. The taste and texture is deeper and more intense, and the fat is richer in flavour.

Clear broth: Parboiling the bones before use removes any impurities, ensuring the end result of the broth is clear. Don't worry, you are not discarding any flavour. Only when the bones are simmered slowly over a low heat will their intense flavour be extracted.

Long and slow simmering: Many hours of simmering over a low heat is key to a clear and flavoursome broth. Avoid moving the ingredients around or even stirring the broth as this causes the ingredients to break up, producing a cloudy broth. Don't rush. Plan your time well and leave plenty of time to ensure perfect results.

Char the onions and ginger: The incredible smoky flavour of charred onion and ginger will add depth of flavour to the broth. There are no shortcuts for this step.

Roast the spices: This will extract maximum flavour and help to create that aromatic taste.

Yellow rock sugar: This smooths the rough edges of the broth by lightly sweetening it, as opposed to granulated sugar where the sweetness is sharper.

Taste: Adding extra water to dilute the broth at the final stage will depend on your tastes. If it's too salty, you will need to balance it out with more water.

Serve hot: Pho should be hot enough to just cook the raw topside beef, which is added when serving. It must be eaten quickly before the noodles get soggy!

Fresh herbs: Their aroma and lightness complement the broth perfectly.

Beef Pho Southern Style

Phở Bò Miền Nam

Beef pho is our national dish and so synonymous with Vietnamese cuisine that the quality of your broth goes a long way to defining you as a chef! Like many Vietnamese classics, the flavours will vary greatly depending on where in the country you are from. As I'm from the Mekong Delta, the recipe I've written here is the southern style, which is closest to my heart. Tweaked over generations to suit the tastebuds of loved ones, this is the recipe I have worked on since the launch of The Little Viet Kitchen and is one that I'm proud to share with you here.

On an open gas flame, char the onions and ginger until the skins are blackened. If you don't have a gas stovetop, then roast in an oven preheated to 180°C/160°C Fan/Gas Mark 4 for 20–25 minutes. Remove, allow to cool enough to handle, then peel the skins off. Rinse in cold water and set aside.

Dry toast all the spices in a small frying pan for 3–5 minutes over a medium heat, until aromatic. Take the pan off the heat and leave to cool. Put the spices into a spice strainer (breaking up the cinnamon stick if necessary) and set aside.

Next, prepare the bones and meat. Squeeze the juice of the lemons into a stockpot, throw the lemon halves in and fill with plenty of cold water. Soak the oxtail, marrow, beef brisket, flank and ribs and bones in the water, then add the salt. Stir well and leave for 1 hour.

Discard the lemon halves and set the pot over a high heat and parboil the bones and meat for 5 minutes. Drain, rinse in cold water and leave to dry.

Rinse the pot used for cleaning the bones and meat and fill with 8 litres of water. Add the par-boiled meat. Blast at extremely high heat for 3–4 minutes to force all the impurities to the surface, then skim off the scum until the water looks clear. Reduce the heat to low, partially cover with the lid and simmer for 3 hours.

Add the prepared onions and ginger along with the daikon to the broth along with 120g salt. Stir in the sugar, then continue to simmer for a further 2 hours. Carefully remove the daikon and onion from the broth, add the spice strainer along with the fish sauce. Cook for a further 3 hours.

Taste and adjust the seasoning to your preference. In the north of Vietnam pho is a little saltier, and in the south it is a little sweeter.

Take the pot off the heat, remove the bones and meat, and allow to cool. Skim off any fat that has risen to the surface, then carefully and slowly strain the broth through a large sieve into a clean stockpot. Don't rush this process if you want to produce that signature clarity to the broth.

Serves 10

3 onions, skins on
200g ginger, unpeeled
2 tablespoons fish sauce
500g dried pho noodles
150g bean sprouts
500g topside steak, thinly sliced

For the spices
10 star anise
5g cloves
3 teaspoons coriander seeds
2 teaspoons fennel seeds
3 cardamom pods, lightly
    crushed, pods discarded and
    seeds only
1 cinnamon stick

For cleaning the meat
2 lemons, halved
5 tablespoons salt

For the broth
500g oxtail
500g beef marrow, chopped into
    7cm pieces (ask the butcher
    to do this)
2kg beef brisket on the bone
500g beef flank
500g beef ribs
1 daikon, peeled and halved
120g salt
200g yellow rock sugar or rock
    sugar, crushed

continued on page 88...

Soak the noodles in a bowl of cold water for 30–45 minutes. Drain and set aside.

For the meat, debone and tear the brisket meat into strips. Cut the flank into thin slices. If you like, tear the meat off the ribs, or serve it on the bones.

Bring a saucepan of water to the boil, then blanch the bean sprouts for 5–10 seconds and drain. Divide the bean sprouts between serving bowls.

Fill the pan with fresh water and cook the soaked noodles for 3–5 seconds, then drain and add to the bowls with the bean sprouts. Add the assortment of cooked meat, then arrange the slices of topside steak on top.

Bring the broth to the boil and ladle between bowls. Add the marrow to the bowls, or leave on the side for guests to help themselves. Finish with the herbs and serve with lime wedges and sriracha and hoisin sauces for dipping the meat.*

Finally, enjoy your first spoonful of broth… You deserve it chef!

Do not add the sauces into the broth. Think of the hours you have spent perfecting it.

To serve
200g coriander leaves
200g spring onions, chopped
200g Thai basil leaves
200g sawtooth herb (optional)
4 limes, cut into wedges
5 bird's eye chillies, sliced
sriracha sauce, for dipping
hoisin sauce, for dipping

Chicken Pho

Phở Gà

Light and fragrant, chicken pho is the little sister of the more complex beef pho, but in no way inferior. Delicately spiced, the tender chicken and hot aromatic broth serves as a hearty breakfast meal to many Vietnamese every day. Taking less than half the cooking time of beef pho, this is my go-to option for a quick pho fix when the need strikes (which, as a Viet, is often).

The subtlety of the flavours makes this a winner for kids as well. I always loved it growing up and watching my nieces and nephew slurping a bowl down never fails to warm my heart. I hope they will grow up loving it as much as I do and maybe one day make it for their children too.

Roast the onions and ginger for approximately 5 minutes directly over an open flame, until you see the juice of the onion bubbling on the surface and the ginger is fully blackened. Wash under cold water and rub the blackened outer layers away.

In a dry pan, roast the star anise and coriander seeds over a medium heat for 2 minutes.

Bring 3 litres of water to the boil in a large stockpot and add the whole chicken, the daikon and the roasted onions and ginger. Place the roasted spices into a spice strainer and position it carefully at the bottom of the pot. Lower the heat and simmer for 1 hour, skimming away any foam that comes to the surface.

Remove the chicken and place to one side to cool. Strain the broth, discarding the solids, and return to the pot. Add the fish sauce, sugar and salt to the broth and simmer for 30 minutes.

Meanwhile, soak the noodles in lukewarm water for 20 minutes. Drain. Bring a pan of water to the boil and cook the noodles for 3–5 seconds. Drain well and leave to cool.

Remove the top and bottom of the spring onions and slice very thinly lengthwise. Soak in a bowl of cold water for 5 minutes until they curl up.

Take a handful of noodles and place into a bowl, and top with a small handful of bean sprouts. Tear the chicken into large chunks and place on top. Now ladle the broth into the bowl leaving some room for adding the herbs. Drain the spring onions and place a few on top of the chicken. Sprinkle over a couple of slices of chilli, the basil leaves and crispy fried shallots. Repeat with the remaining bowls.

Lastly squeeze a lime quarter into each bowl to balance the flavours of the broth. Serve with hoisin and sriracha dipping sauce, and extra lime for squeezing.

Serves 4–6

200g dried pho noodles
6 spring onions
500g bean sprouts
2 red chillies, sliced
large handful of Thai basil
handful of Crispy Fried Shallots
  (page 25)
2 limes, quartered
2 teaspoons hoisin sauce
2 teaspoons sriracha sauce

For the broth
2 onions, unpeeled
20g piece ginger, unpeeled
5 star anise
1 teaspoon coriander seeds
1 whole chicken, approx 1.3kg
18cm piece daikon, peeled
3 tablespoons fish sauce
50g rock sugar, crushed
1 teaspoon salt

Crab, Pork and Tomato Noodle Soup

Bún Riêu Cua Giò Heo

I have so much love for this dish that when I first started planning the recipes for the book, it was first on my list to share with you. A little bowl of heaven that will always remind me of grandma. Every so often at the morning market you would hear the call of 'fresh crabs, who wants to buy fresh crabs?'. I knew it could mean bún riêu for dinner, but only if I could find grandma in time before the other chefs in the village bought them all. I would run as fast as my little legs would allow me and then breathlessly and excitedly relay the news! Then back to the market we would go, me dragging her by her áo bà ba shirt pocket, in the hope that this would help her speed. She would pretend to scold me for being too excited, but there was always a little glint in her eyes that told me she was glad I ran to tell her. Happiness through feeding loved ones never needs words and never needs an explanation. I have always seen this in my mum and I feel it in myself today.

Below is the recipe for the traditional and authentic bún riêu, but every now and then I like to add my own twist. If you're feeling luxurious add jumbo prawns and crab claws to the broth at the same time as the crab and pork balls (you'll need one of each per serving).

To make the broth, first prepare some shrimp paste water. Combine the shrimp paste and the boiling water in a bowl and mix well to dissolve. Leave to infuse for 3 hours and then strain through a fine sieve, keeping the water to add to the broth later. Discard any solids.

While the shrimp paste water is infusing, bring plenty of water to the boil in a large saucepan. Add the pig's trotters and 1 teaspoon of salt, and cook for 1½ hours. Drain, rinse the trotters under cold running water, drain again, then set aside.

Fill the same pan with water again and bring to the boil. Add the pork leg and pork bones, boiling them together for 5 minutes. Take off the heat, rinse under cold running water, drain again and set aside.

Bring 8 litres of water to the boil in a stockpot over a high heat. Add the pork trotters, leg and bones, carrots, onions and daikon. Bring the water back to the boil and skim the surface to remove the impurities. Lower the heat and simmer for 1 hour. Remove the vegetables from the pot and continue to simmer for a further hour.

In the meantime, make the riêu sauce. In a saucepan over a medium heat, add all the riêu sauce ingredients and stir to warm through for 5–6 minutes, but do not let the mixture boil. Pour the sauce into a bowl, allow to cool and set aside while you make the crab and pork mixture.

Serves 10–12

For the broth

2 tablespoons shrimp paste
400ml boiling water
1kg pig's trotters
150g salt, plus 2 teaspoons
1kg pork leg pieces
1kg pork bone pieces
2 carrots, peeled
2 onions, peeled
1 daikon, peeled and halved
150g salt, plus 2 teaspoons
300g rock sugar, crushed
2 tablespoons fish sauce
400g Deep-fried Tofu (page 25), cubed

For the riêu sauce

6 garlic cloves, finely diced
1 medium onion, diced
4 spring onions, finely chopped
3 tablespoons tomato purée

Bring a saucepan of water to the boil. Add the crab and blanch for 20–25 minutes. Drain. When cool enough to handle, remove the shell, keeping the crabmeat and roe. Place in a bowl along with the pork mince, salt, sugar, peppercorns and fish sauce. Mix well and, once cooled, combine with the riêu sauce and finely chopped shrimp, then add the eggs to help bind. Shape the crab and pork mixture into balls and set aside.

Once the broth has simmered for 2 hours in total, remove the pork leg and trotters. Slice the pork leg thinly and set the leg meat aside on a chopping board.

Now add the crab and pork balls, 150g salt, rock sugar, fish sauce and shrimp paste water to the broth, then taste. Add more seasoning if needed and simmer for a further hour.

Meanwhile, prepare the tomatoes. Heat the oil in a saucepan and place over a medium heat. Add the shallots and the cherry tomatoes, stir-fry until the shallots turn golden, then add the strained tinned tomatoes. Continue to stir-fry for 5–6 minutes, until the tomatoes have broken down. Take off the heat and set aside, keep warm until serving.

Make the dipping sauce by combining the fish sauce with the chillies in a small bowl. Set aside.

Once the crab and pork balls have simmered in the broth for 1 hour, and the broth has been cooking for 3 hours in total, prepare the noodles by following the packet instructions, and add the tofu to the broth for a final 10 minutes of cooking.

To serve, divide the bean sprouts between bowls, top with the noodles, then arrange a few pieces of pork leg and some of the chả lụa ham. The pig's trotters can be added to the bowl at this point or left on the side, depending on preference.

Ladle the broth over the noodles, not forgetting to include a few pieces of tofu and the deliciously fluffy crab and pork balls to each bowl. Top with some juicy tomatoes too.

This dish is to be enjoyed with wedges of lime, the chillies, spring onions and an abundance of herbs, so add them to your heart's content.

320g brown crabmeat, minced
50g cinnamon sticks
2 tablespoons Annatto Seed Oil (page 22), made using sesame oil in place of the vegetable oil

For the crab and pork mixture
1 large whole crab
200g pork mince
1 teaspoon salt
1 teaspoon granulated sugar
1 teaspoon black peppercorns
1 teaspoon fish sauce
200g dried shrimp, soaked in warm water for 30 minutes, drained and finely chopped
6 large eggs, beaten

For the tomatoes
2 tablespoons vegetable oil
8 Asian shallots, thinly sliced
1kg cherry tomatoes
400g tin plum tomatoes, strained

For the dipping sauce
15ml fish sauce per serving
6 bird's eye chillies, sliced

To serve
500g dried vermicelli noodles
150g bean sprouts, soaked in hot water for about 20 seconds, then drained
400g chả lụa Vietnamese ham, thinly sliced
2 limes, cut into wedges
6 bird's eye chillies, cut into diagonal slices
200g spring onions, finely chopped
200g coriander, torn or roughly chopped
200g perilla leaves, torn or finely chopped
200g mint leaves
200g banana blossom, finely sliced
200g raw morning glory (optional)

Hanoi Noodle Soup with Chicken, Pork and Egg

Bún Thang

A very simple broth but one that retains all the drama and intensity of a classic noodle bowl. The dish originates from northern Vietnam but is made all over the country.

To make the broth, bring 6 litres of water to the boil in a stockpot over a high heat. Add the chicken, pork ribs, carcass and bones along with the onions and daikon. Skim the impurities from the surface of the water, then lower the heat and simmer for 30 minutes. Take out the chicken breasts and leave on a chopping board until cool enough to handle. Shred the chicken and set aside in the fridge.

Season the broth with salt, fish sauce and rock sugar, then continue to cook for a further 45 minutes. Remove the carcass and bones along with the daikon and onions, then leave the broth to simmer for a further 15 minutes.

To prepare the toppings, soak the shiitake mushrooms in a bowl of hot water for 1 hour. Drain and pat dry with paper towels, then slice very thinly. Set aside.

Soak the shrimp in a bowl of warm water for 30 minutes, then drain. Blitz in a food processor until you have a fine floss and set aside.

Bring a saucepan of water to the boil and add the prawns. Blanch for 2–3 minutes, drain and set aside.

Wash the pan, add 1 tablespoon of oil and set over a medium heat. Add the pork, salt, sugar, fish sauce, black peppercorns, turmeric and spring onions. Mix well and fry for 8–10 minutes.

Heat a little of the remaining oil in a large frying pan over a medium heat. Add a third of the beaten eggs, tilting the pan to form a thin layer of egg and fry until cooked. Remove and repeat with the remaining eggs to make 3 thin omelettes. Very finely slice and set aside.

Next, bring a saucepan of water to the boil and cook the noodles according to the packet instructions. Drain and rinse in cold water to stop the noodles from cooking further.

To serve, add a handful of noodles to the bottom of each serving bowl. Place a small portion of each topping over the noodles and add a teaspoon of the shrimp to each bowl. Sprinkle over the fresh herbs.

Bring the broth back up to the boil and then ladle into the bowls.

On a side plate for each bowl add a wedge of lime, a few extra slices of chillies and some more shrimp paste on the side, to add to your diners' tastes.

Serves 6–8

400g packet dried thick
    rice noodles

For the broth
500g chicken breast fillets
300g pork ribs
1kg chicken carcass and bones
2 onions, peeled
1 daikon, peeled and halved
1 teaspoon salt
1 teaspoon fish sauce
30g rock sugar, crushed

For the toppings
8 dried shiitake mushrooms
5 tablespoons dried shrimp
16 raw king prawns, deveined
    and peeled
250g minced pork
3 tablespoons vegetable oil
1 teaspoon salt
3 teaspoons granulated sugar
1 teaspoon fish sauce
1 teaspoon crushed black
    peppercorns
½ teaspoon turmeric
5 spring onions, finely chopped
6 eggs, beaten
400g chả lụa Vietnamese ham, cut
    into fine matchsticks

To serve (optional)
100g spring onions, finely chopped
100g coriander, finely chopped
100g Vietnamese mint, finely
    chopped
100g white onions, cut into fine
    matchsticks
Crispy Fried Shallots (page 25)
100g bird's eye chillies, thinly
    sliced on the diagonal
lime wedges

Pork and Seafood Noodle Soup

Hủ Tiếu Nam Vang

I am often asked what the classic dish of southern Vietnam is, and when I reply 'hủ tiếu', I tend to get blank looks. It seems that not many people have heard of it, which is such a shame as it's one of the most wonderful dishes that Vietnam has to offer. It's light and fresh, bursting with flavour and full of different textures and tastes. It's one of those dishes that every time I eat it I swear it's my favourite and can't believe I don't have it more often.

It's such a perfect combination, a beautiful fusion of influences from Cambodia, China and of course Vietnam. As if one country was not complicated enough, right? Well, trust me it is well worth it. This is a dish where I have seen so many different toppings, and they always work. As long as you get the broth right, the bowl is your oyster.

There are two ways this dish can be made, a wet and a dry version. My recipe is for the wet version, although to make it in the dry style you would still follow the recipe here but simply pour the broth into a separate bowl to serve on the side. Then all you need to do is make the soy caramel sauce detailed below, pour that over the dry ingredients in the bowl and voilà.

Fill a stockpot with water and bring to the boil over a high heat. Add the pork ribs and boil for 3–5 minutes. Wash in cold water and drain.

Heat 6 litres fresh water in the pot and add the pork ribs and loin. Bring to the boil over a high heat and skim away the impurities on the surface. Reduce the heat to low and simmer for 30 minutes.

Take the pork loin out of the broth, leaving the ribs behind. Add the daikon, onions, salted turnip, dried squid and dried shrimp. Bring back up to the boil, skim away the impurities on the surface of the broth and reduce the heat to low. Simmer for 1 hour. Add the sugar and salt, and simmer for a further 30 minutes. Then add the fish sauce and simmer for a further 10 minutes. Take the pot off the heat and set aside.

Heat the oil in a saucepan over a medium heat. Add the minced pork, salt, sugar, peppercorns and spring onions, and stir-fry for 4–5 minutes until the pork is browned and cooked. Take off the heat and leave to cool down on the side.

Finely chop the garlic chives, spring onions, coriander and Chinese celery. Put into a bowl and mix well, then set aside.

Bring a saucepan of water to the boil and cook the noodles for 5–8 minutes, until al dente. (Do follow the instructions on the packet as timings can vary slightly between brands.) Take off the heat and immediately rinse the noodles

Serves 6–8

400g packet hủ tiếu tapioca
   noodles
1 teaspoon vegetable oil, for
   the noodles
16 king prawns, deveined
   and peeled
200g calamari, sliced into 1cm
   wide rings
200g pig's liver
16 crab claws
300g bean sprouts
16 hard-boiled quail's eggs or
   6–8 hen's eggs

For the broth
1kg pork ribs
1kg cooked pork loin, cut into
   thin slices
1 daikon, peeled and halved
2 onions, peeled
100g dried salted turnip

in cold water to stop them from cooking further. To prevent the noodles sticking together, add the oil to the palms of your hands and run your fingers through the noodles. Set aside.

If making the dry version of this recipe, make the soy caramel sauce. Heat the soy sauce and sugar in a small frying pan over the lowest possible heat, until caramelised and syrupy. Take the pan off the heat and set aside.

Prepare the prawns and calamari by bringing a saucepan of water to the boil. Add the prawns and calamari and blanch for 2–3 minutes. Drain and set aside.

Bring a saucepan of water to the boil and add the pig's liver. Blanch for 10 minutes, then drain. Plunge the liver in iced water and leave for 5 minutes. Drain and thinly slice. Do the same with the crab claws but do not slice them.

Wash the pan and fill with water. Bring the water to the boil over a high heat, add the bean sprouts and blanch for 5 minutes. Remove from the heat and drain.

To assemble, put a small handful of bean sprouts at the bottom of each serving bowl. Add the noodles, then top with slices of pork, liver, crab claws, calamari, prawns, eggs and a spoonful of pork mince.

If using, bring the broth back up to the boil and pour into the bowls.

If making the dry version, add the soy caramel sauce and toss the ingredients together. The broth can be served on the side in a small bowl.

Lastly, add the crispy fried shallots, crispy garlic and crushed peppercorns, and garnish with the fresh herbs. Serve with lime wedges for squeezing and a few chilli slices on top will provide that perfect kick.

50g dried squid, rinsed in cold water, drained and patted dry with paper towels
50g dried shrimp, rinsed in cold water, drained and patted dry with paper towels
300g rock sugar, crushed
2 tablespoons salt
1 tablespoon fish sauce

For the soy caramel sauce (optional)
2 tablespoons soy sauce
6 tablespoons granulated sugar

For the pork mince topping
1 tablespoon vegetable oil
500g minced pork
½ teaspoon salt
½ teaspoon granulated sugar
1 teaspoon crushed black peppercorns
4 spring onions, whites only, finely chopped

To serve
100g garlic chives
100g spring onions
100g coriander
100g Chinese celery
Crispy Fried Shallots (page 25)
Crispy Garlic (page 26)
8 teaspoons crushed black peppercorns
2 limes, cut into wedges
6 bird's eye chillies, thinly sliced diagonally

Spicy Beef and Pork Noodles

Bún Bò Huế

A personal favourite, this dish is bursting with aromatic depth and has enough fire to scare dragons. A signature dish from Huế, representing the spicy flavour characteristic of the region and uncommon outside of it.

Traditionally, the noodles would be accompanied with cubes of pork blood and Huế-style pork patties. If you want to make the dish according to Huế style simply add these to the finished broth before serving. This recipe doesn't include them though as personally I prefer the broth without.

Don't be put off by the quantities in the recipe. It's a family dish so needs to be made in large amounts. You can freeze the broth for up to three months.

First, make the shrimp paste water. Combine the 2 tablespoons of shrimp paste with the just-boiled water. Mix well to dissolve, then set aside for 3 hours. Strain the mixture through a fine sieve, keeping only the water and leaving it aside for later.

Next, squeeze the juice of the lemons into a stockpot filled with plenty of cold water, then place the squeezed lemon halves in too. Add the oxtail, pork ribs, beef shin, beef shank, pork leg and beef brisket along with the salt. Stir well and set aside for 1 hour, then wash and drain.

For the broth, heat the vegetable oil in a saucepan over a medium heat. When hot, add the cinnamon, cloves, garlic, ginger and lemongrass, and toss for 5–6 minutes until aromatic and golden. Take off the heat and leave to cool.

Bring plenty of water to the boil in a stockpot, add the meat and cook over a high heat for 3–4 minutes. Skim the impurities from the surface of the liquid, then take the pot off the heat and drain. Wash the meat in cold water, pat dry with paper towels and set aside.

Refill the stockpot with 8 litres fresh water and add the par-boiled meat. Bring the water up to the boil, skimming away any impurities. Reduce the heat to low and simmer for 1 hour. Add the cinnamon, cloves, garlic, ginger and lemongrass mixture, then continue to simmer the broth for 3 hours.

Meanwhile, heat the sesame oil in a small saucepan over a medium heat and add the annatto seeds. Sauté for 2–3 minutes, until the oil turns red from the annatto seeds. Strain the oil into a bowl and discard the seeds. Pour the oil back into the pan and add the garlic and shallots. Heat the oil over a medium–low heat and fry for 2–3 minutes until the garlic is golden and the shallots are translucent. Take the pan off the heat and set aside until needed.

To make the shrimp chilli sauce, heat the vegetable oil in a saucepan over a medium heat. Add the garlic, lemongrass and chillies, stirring until the garlic is golden. Add the dried chilli flakes and shrimp paste. Stir well and then remove

Serves 15

2 tablespoons shrimp paste
400ml just-boiled water
2 lemons, halved
1kg oxtail, chopped into 5cm dice
500g pork ribs
500g beef shin
500g beef shank
1kg pork leg
500g beef brisket
5 tablespoons salt
4 tablespoons sesame oil
3 tablespoons annatto seeds
5 garlic cloves, finely chopped
8 shallots, finely sliced
750g thick vermicelli rice noodles, cooked according to the packet instructions

For the broth

2 tablespoons vegetable oil
2 small cinnamon sticks
4 cloves
3 garlic cloves
150g ginger, skin on, cut into 2cm thick slices
10 lemongrass stalks, crushed
½ ripe pineapple, peeled and sliced into 2cm thick discs
1 daikon, peeled and roughly chopped
3 onions, peeled

the pan from the heat. Immediately pour in the sesame oil – this will help cool the sauce down quickly, preventing the ingredients from cooking further. Set aside.

Once the broth has simmered for 3 hours, remove the beef shin, beef shank, pork leg and oxtail from the broth and transfer to a baking tray. Allow to cool and then transfer the meat to the fridge while you finish off the broth.

Top up with more water if needed, and add the pineapple, daikon, and onions to the broth, then continue to simmer for a further 4½ hours. Take out the brisket (and set aside) and pork ribs (set aside if you want to serve these), and add the shrimp paste water, sugar, salt, fish sauce and the reserved garlic and shallot annatto seed oil. Stir in about 3 tablespoons of the shrimp chilli sauce and add more or less depending on taste. Simmer for a further 30 minutes, and taste again, adjusting the level of seasoning. Keep warm.

Thinly slice the pork leg, beef shin and beef shank. Tear the beef brisket into strips, remembering to tear along the grain. The pork ribs can be served but all their goodness was extracted during the making of the broth.

To serve, place a handful of the bean sprouts, the noodles, 3 pieces of each meat and 1 oxtail into each bowl. Ladle over the hot broth and garnish with the fresh herbs, chillies and, if using, the perilla leaves, morning glory and banana blossoms. Add a little of the chả lụa Vietnamese ham to each bowl and have a couple wedges of lime for squeezing on the side to add a zesty kick.

Now, sit back and eat like no one is watching!

300g rock sugar, crushed
200g salt
3 tablespoons fish sauce

For the shrimp chilli sauce
100ml vegetable oil
100g garlic, finely minced
4 lemongrass stalks, very
    finely chopped
100g bird's eye chillies,
    finely chopped
30g dried chilli flakes
2 tablespoons shrimp paste
100ml sesame oil

To serve
200g bean sprouts
200g Thai basil leaves
200g coriander stems
100g spring onions, chopped
3–5 bird's eye chillies, sliced
200g perilla leaves (optional)
200g morning glory (optional)
200g banana blossoms (optional)
400g chả lụa Vietnamese ham,
    thinly sliced
2 limes, cut into wedges

Street
Food

Street Food

When I was little, I never went to a restaurant, but I never needed or wanted to, as I loved everything the market offered and represented. Food doesn't have to be expensive, just full of enticing aromas, bursting with flavours that spark your memories and, most importantly, are made with love and care. When I visit a Vietnamese street market today I find myself totally immersed in the sights, sounds and aromas. I find it impossible not to be hungry … even just thinking about it now!

Markets open early in Vietnam, often at 5 or 6am, so you have to be there early to get the best ingredients or the juiciest dishes. If you arrive at 8am you're too late! Traditionally, generations of the same family will have been at the same spot, making the same delicious dish for many years. Each street food stall is like a mini restaurant, with the 'head chef' expertly skilled in making their dish with as much love, effort and pride as they can.

Being what I call 'food proud' is such a vital part of Vietnamese culture and nowhere is this seen more than at the market. Vendors are known for their dish and most stalls will only make one thing, but they will make it perfectly. You'd go to auntie #6 for your favourite spring rolls, and auntie #8 for your favourite bánh mì. It's their dish, their signature, and no one else at the market would make it. Each stallholder is so proud of what they make; the love of feeding and sharing is so bound up in our culture. The aunties will always offer as much as possible to whoever buys from them, stuffing in as many goodies as they can. So as you can imagine, when I was little, I'd always manage to negotiate a little extra!

The market is a huge part of rural life in Vietnam, where the nearest supermarket is often very far away. The village market where I grew up, like many others around the country, is essentially a large communal kitchen, made for sharing. I often think it's like getting the best bits from many different family meals, and I have always loved the idea of having several little bites of lots of different things!

To me, the traditional Vietnamese street food market represents life; it's where everything happens, from the major to the trivial. It's where the whole community meets every day, to buy, sell and barter their goods. It's where they socialise, drink tea and put the world to rights; it's where they sell what they've grown on their farms or made in their kitchens and where they buy the groceries that will feed their families that day.

Family, home and food are at the heart of Vietnamese culture and the markets are completely bound up in this. The market is where hard work, drive, fun, love and passion all come together, and my overwhelming memory is happiness. And of course the wonderful foods that inspire so much of my work today.

Growing up in Vietnam we didn't have much and my mum worked hard every day just to feed us, so we never had much to spend at the market. When you know you can only have one sugar cane prawn cake a month, you really make the most of it, savouring each and every bite. Just like when you steal that piece of meat from a big family meal just before it's served… It's always the best mouthful you will eat!

I remember the market as being such a hospitable and happy place, with a strong sense of community, in which everyone played an important role. You would sit at your stall until you'd sold everything, as you'd know that unless you did, you and your family wouldn't be eating very well that day. So until you'd sold everything, you couldn't move on to the rest of your day, which would be filled with looking after your family and home, tending the farm and animals and preparing for the next day's market. Within the community there was always a strong sense of support and camaraderie, so families would do all they could to help each other. Often you would end up buying something you didn't really need, just to help auntie #3 and her family.

The recipes in this chapter are full of the delicious flavours I used to find at my local market; I hope you love them as much as I did!

Vietnamese Baguettes

Bánh Mì

Bánh mì is classic Vietnamese street food. Fill yours with anything you like, but I've suggested my favourite fillings.

Preheat the oven to 180°C/160°C Fan/Gas Mark 4. Warm the baguette in the over for 2–3 minutes.

Remove the baguette from the oven and cut it down the centre. Pull out enough of the insides of the baguette to make enough room for the fillings.

Spread the butter on one side of the baguette, then spread the mayonnaise on top. On the other side, spread the pâté.

Lay the cucumber inside the baguette followed by the pickled carrot and daikon, and a generous amount of your chosen filling. Add the coriander and the spring onion and drizzle over the soy sauce.

Lastly, sprinkle with chilli slices, crispy fried shallots and crushed black peppercorns.

Serves 1

1 baguette
2 teaspoons butter
3 teaspoons Mayonnaise (page 30)
4 teaspoons chicken liver pâté
1 cucumber, seeds removed and
  cut into thick slices
20g Pickled Carrot and Daikon
  (page 23)
choice of fillings (below and page
  113)
2 stems coriander
1 spring onion, sliced lengthways
2 teaspoons soy sauce
¼ red chilli, sliced
1 teaspoon Crispy Fried Shallots
  (page 25)
pinch of crushed black peppercorns

Lemongrass Chicken Bánh Mì Filling

Bánh Mì Thịt Gà Xào Sả Ớt

Combine the chicken with the ingredients for the marinade in a large bowl. Leave in the fridge to marinate for at least 3 hours, or ideally overnight for perfect results.

Heat the oil in a frying pan over a medium heat until it reaches 160°C. An easy way to tell when the oil is ready is to place a wooden chopstick into it – when bubbles form on the surface of the oil it is ready.

Add the chicken strips and all of the marinade to the pan, and stir-fry for 10–12 minutes, or until the chicken is golden in colour and cooked through. Keep the chicken moving at all times as the sugar in the marinade can burn easily.

Take the pan off the heat and put the chicken straight into your bánh mì.

Makes enough to fill 4 baguettes

750g chicken breast fillets, sliced
  diagonally into 1 × 5cm strips
2 tablespoons vegetable oil

For the marinade
2 teaspoons soy sauce
1 teaspoon fish sauce
1 teaspoon oyster sauce
1 tablespoon granulated sugar
1 teaspoon honey
2 tablespoons finely diced
  lemongrass stalks
2 tablespoons finely diced garlic
1 tablespoon finely diced chillies
1 tablespoon finely diced onion
4 tablespoons sesame oil

Pork Belly Bánh Mì Filling

Bánh Mì Thịt Heo Nướng Xả Ớt

Thinly slice the pork belly into 5cm × 0.5cm strips, then put into a large bowl along with ingredients for the marinade. Mix everything together well and leave in the fridge to marinate for a minimum of 3 hours, or ideally overnight for perfect results.

Take the pork strips and thread them onto the skewers, piece by piece. Don't put too many pieces on one skewer otherwise they won't cook evenly.

Preheat the oven to 180°C/160°C Fan/Gas Mark 4 and line a baking sheet with baking parchment. Place the skewers on the prepared baking sheet, setting aside the remaining marinade. Cook in the oven for 10 minutes, then turn the skewers over and continue to cook for a further 10 minutes.

Pour all of the excess marinade over the skewers and cook for a further 5 minutes, then remove from the oven.

Use a fork to strip the pork from the skewers directly into your bánh mì. Scrumptious.

Makes enough to fill 4 baguettes

750g pork belly
12 bamboo skewers, soaked in cold water for 20 minutes

For the marinade
1 teaspoon soy sauce
2 teaspoons fish sauce
1 teaspoon oyster sauce
1 tablespoon granulated sugar
1 tablespoon honey
2 tablespoons Chilli and Lemongrass Marinade (page 21)
2 tablespoons finely diced lemongrass stalks
2 tablespoons finely diced garlic
1 tablespoon finely diced onion
4 tablespoons sesame oil

Lemongrass Fried Tofu Mì Filling

Bánh Mì Tàu Hũ Chiên Xả Ớt

Place the tofu in a bowl.

Heat the vegetable oil in a frying pan over a medium heat until it reaches 160°C. An easy way to tell when the oil is ready is to place a wooden chopstick into it – when bubbles form on the surface of the oil it is ready.

Add the garlic and lemongrass, and fry for 2 minutes until golden brown. Add the remaining ingredients, except the tofu, and stir-fry for a further 3 minutes.

Take the pan off the heat and pour the sauce over the tofu. Set aside to cool, then gently run your fingers through the mix to evenly coat all the tofu strips with the sauce. Now stuff the tofu straight into your bánh mì.

Makes enough to fill 4 baguettes

400g Deep-fried Tofu (page 25)
2 tablespoons vegetable oil
1 tablespoon finely diced garlic
1 tablespoon finely diced lemongrass stalk
2 teaspoons soy sauce
2 teaspoons mushroom oyster sauce
1 tablespoon granulated sugar
1 tablespoon honey
1 tablespoon finely chopped red chillies
1 tablespoon finely diced onion
3 tablespoons sesame oil

Prawn Patties on Sugar Cane Sticks

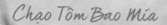

Chạo Tôm Bao Mía

This is probably the only dish that I'm excited to finish eating. Strange but true, and all because when you've finished you get to chew on a deliciously juicy sweet sugar cane, still infused with all the herbs and flavours of the prawns. The joy on children's faces when eating this is just priceless. It's like a Kinder Egg, but instead of a toy inside, it's another Kinder Egg! Who would complain?

When it comes to street food, there are some dishes that will stay with you forever. For me it never has to be expensive or fancy, just full of flavours that take you back in time and bursting with aromas that stick with you wherever you go. Well, this dish definitely does that for me.

Sugar cane is cheap and cheerful on the Mekong Delta. Along with coconut, it is our go-to sweet option. So chewing on a stick or two as a snack was very normal growing up.

The juice is freshly squeezed at the market, put into a small clear plastic bag with a straw through the top and then tied with a bright rubber band. Unfortunately it is impossible to get in London, and the canned import is really not the same. But that just helps to make it an extra special treat whenever I go back to visit my grandparents.

So, let's get started, the sooner you make this, the sooner you will know what I mean.

continued on page 118...

Prawn Patties on Sugar Cane Sticks...

First, make the prawn mixture. Combine all the ingredients in a food processor and blitz for 25–30 seconds. Transfer to a bowl and place in the fridge for at least 3 hours, or overnight if you can for a really good springy texture.

Divide the mixture into 12 portions of around 60g each. Very lightly oil both your hands with some of the sesame oil. Take one portion of the mixture, roll it into a ball, then press the ball flat to form a round patty. Repeat with the remaining mixture, oiling your hands as needed.

Place one sugar cane stick on top of the centre of one of the patties so that it overhangs on each side, then wrap the patty firmly around the sugar cane and smooth over to join. Use your palm to keep moulding the prawns into a ball. Use even more oil on your hands as this will help smooth out the mixture. The shape does not have to be perfect, as long as the prawn mixture sticks to the sugar cane. Repeat this process for the remaining patties and sugar cane sticks.

You can choose to grill or deep-fry these. Personally, I prefer them deep-fried but a healthier but still tasty option would be to grill them.

To deep-fry, heat the vegetable oil in a large pan or saucepan over a medium heat until it reaches 160°C. An easy way to tell when the oil is ready is to place a wooden chopstick into it – when bubbles form on the surface of the oil it is ready. Add the skewers and fry for 2–3 minutes, until golden and crispy (the time will depend on how big you've made your prawn patties).

To grill the skewers, preheat the grill and line a tray with foil. Cook the skewers for 2–3 minutes, rotating them until you feel they're cooked through and golden.

There are a few different ways to serve cháo tôm bao mía. On their own as a starter or snack with my tomato sauce (page 31), or alternatively, serve them atop bowls of vermicelli rice noodle with plenty of fresh herbs and classic fish dipping sauce (page 28). They are also delicious taken off the cane, wrapped in rice paper to make a summer roll.

Makes 12

5 tablespoons sesame oil

12 fresh sugar cane sticks, or defrosted if frozen

1.5 litres vegetable oil

For the prawn mixture

500g raw prawns, peeled and deveined

1 tablespoon finely chopped lemongrass stalks

1 teaspoon finely chopped red chilli

1 tablespoon crushed black peppercorns

4 spring onions, finely chopped

2 teaspoons granulated sugar

1 teaspoon salt

1 tablespoon cornflour

1 teaspoon fish sauce

3 tablespoons sesame oil

2 egg whites, beaten

Crispy Pork and Prawn Spring Rolls

Chả Giò Tôm Thịt Heo

Filled with wonderfully seasoned meat and vegetables, these heavenly rolls should be golden in colour and both crunchy and chewy on the bite. A clear, thin transparent rice paper is the traditional one to use; however as this is not the easiest to control you may find it easier to start with the Chinese-style slightly thicker paper. Either way, patience and practice are the secret ingredients in this recipe. Have faith, don't give up, because even if they do split occasionally, they are still absolutely delicious!

Soak the noodles in a bowl of just-boiled water for 20 minutes. Drain well, pat dry with paper towels and cut into rough 5cm lengths. Do the same with the mushrooms, cutting them into small pieces.

Put the noodles and mushrooms in a large mixing bowl along with the remaining filling ingredients and the egg whites. Mix well, and evenly.

Now get ready to roll. Have a bowl of lukewarm water to wet the rice paper, and a chopping board or plate that is big enough to hold your rice paper for rolling.

Dunk the rice paper into the water very quickly and then lay flat on the board. Leave for about a minute, until almost dry before rolling. An easy way to set up is to work with 3 rolls at once. By the time you have laid the filling out on the third one, the first will be ready to roll.

Place your filling mixture in a line down the centre of the rice paper. Fold each side inwards towards the centre and then fold the paper from the bottom up over the mixture, like an envelope. Press firmly using your fingertips and start folding, be gentle but firm, controlling the movement and not allowing any of the filling to come out, making sure that the roll is tight. Seal by brushing the edges with a little of the reserved egg yolk. Continue to repeat the process until all your ingredients are used up. You should have 16 rolls in total.

Heat the oil in a deep-fat fryer or in a frying large pan to 160°C. An easy way to tell when the oil is ready is to place a wooden chopstick into it – when bubbles form on the surface of the oil it is ready.

Add the spring rolls and deep-fry for 5–6 minutes, until light golden in colour and firm to touch with tongs. Remove and drain on paper towels.

Serve with the classic fish dipping sauce, or your choice of sauces from the first chapter of the book.

Makes 16 rolls

4 eggs, separated
16 rice paper sheets
500ml vegetable oil
Classic Fish Dipping Sauce (page 28), to serve

For the filling
100g dried glass noodles
50g dried black fungus mushrooms
250g minced pork
250g raw king prawns, shells and tails removed, deveined and minced
200g carrots, grated
50g white cabbage, shredded
100g canned water chestnuts, drained and diced
6 spring onions, finely chopped
2 tablespoons granulated sugar
1 tablespoon salt
1 teaspoon fish sauce
2 tablespoons sesame oil
2 tablespoons ground black peppercorns

Tofu and Vegetable Spring Rolls

Chả Giò Chạy Tàu Hũ

As well as adding a smooth and sweet flavour to the filling, the mung beans act as a paste to glue the other ingredients together.

First, prepare the mung beans. Bring 1 litre of water in a saucepan to the boil over a high heat. Add the mung beans and lower the heat to medium. Cover with the lid and cook for 20–25 minutes. Turn the heat to medium-low and simmer for a further 5 minutes, uncovered. Stir occasionally to ensure the beans are evenly cooked. Taste them at this point; the texture should be soft like a paste. Tip into a large bowl.

Add the remaining ingredients for the filling. Use your hands to gently mix everything together.

Now get ready to roll. Have a bowl of lukewarm water to wet the rice paper, and a chopping board or plate that is big enough to hold your rice paper for rolling.

Dunk the rice paper into the water very quickly and then lay flat on the board. Leave for about a minute, until almost dry before rolling. An easy way to set up is to work with 3 rolls at once. By the time you have laid the filling out on the third one, the first will be ready to roll.

Place your filling mixture in a line down the centre of the rice paper. Fold each side inwards towards the centre and then fold the paper from the bottom up over the mixture, like an envelope. Press firmly using your fingertips and start folding, be gentle but firm, controlling the movement and not allowing any of the filling to come out, making sure that the roll is tight. Seal. Continue to repeat the process until all your ingredients are used up. You should have 30 rolls in total.

Heat the oil in a large frying pan over a medium heat until it reaches 160°C. An easy way to tell when the oil is ready is to place a wooden chopstick into it – when bubbles form on the surface of the oil it is ready. Carefully drop a spring roll to test the heat and cooking time; the first one never turns out well so choose a spring roll you don't mind sacrificing. Deep-fry for 5–6 minutes, until golden, crisp and cooked through. Depending on the size of your pan, deep-fry the spring rolls in batches to prevent overcrowding the pan.

These spring rolls are perfect as starters or small plates served alongside the vegan soy dipping sauce. If serving as part of a main meal, simply place atop bowls of vermicelli noodles and some fresh herbs.

Makes approx 30 rolls

30 dried rice paper sheets
2 litres vegetable oil
Vegan Soy Dipping Sauce
(page 30), to serve

For the filling
200g dried mung beans,
soaked in cold water for 30
minutes and rinsed to remove
excess dirt
2 tablespoons sesame oil
1 tablespoon salt
2 tablespoons soy sauce
3 tablespoons granulated sugar
1 tablespoon honey
2 tablespoons crushed
black peppercorns
2 tablespoons finely
chopped garlic
100g dried glass noodles, soaked
in warm water for 30 minutes,
drained, pat dry and cut into
4cm strips
100g water chestnuts, diced then
squeezed in muslin to remove
excess moisture
100g wood ear mushrooms,
soaked in warm water for 30
minutes, drained, patted dry
and shredded
300g white cabbage, shredded
200g carrots, shredded
100g spring onions, white parts
only, diced
400g Deep-fried Tofu (page 25),
finely chopped

Salmon, Mango and Viola Summer Rolls

Gỏi Cuốn Cá Hồi, Xoài Và Hoa Viola

This is my twist on the traditional gỏi cuốn, summer rolls (a traditional recipe follows on page 127). I devised these beautiful summer rolls as a dish for my supper club and I'm so proud when I now see variations all over Instagram, from every corner of the globe. This is one dish that I would encourage you to be as imaginative as you can with, and invent your own variations. Perhaps you like the sound of sashimi tuna and thinly sliced strawberries or beef carpaccio and kiwi fruit?! Be crazy, be creative and tag me on Instagram. I would love to see your efforts!

Have ready a bowl of lukewarm water to wet the rice paper and a chopping board or plate big enough to hold your rice paper for rolling.

Dunk the rice paper into the water very quickly and then lay it flat on the board. Leave for about 1 minute, until almost dry before rolling. A little tip for this is to set up 3 together, so by the time you have laid the filling out on the third one, the first will be ready to roll.

Start by placing 5 viola flowers face down in a line along the centre of each sheet of rice paper, leaving about a 5cm gap on each side. Lay about 20g of smoked salmon neatly over the flowers on each sheet.

Next put a sixth of each of the mango, cucumber, carrot, pepper, mint, coriander and perilla leaves on top of the salmon. As summer rolls are see-through I always think it's worth making sure that all the ingredients are arranged neatly so the finished roll is beautiful.

Now fold each side inwards towards the centre and then fold the paper from the bottom up over the filling, like an envelope. Press firmly using your fingertips and carefully start rolling. Be gentle but firm, controlling the movement and not allowing any of the filling to come out, making sure that the roll is tight.

Repeat the process for the remaining summer rolls. You should have 6 in total. It is always best to serve these immediately, but you can store the rolls for to 2–3 hours in an airtight container to keep them moist.

Traditionally this is served with classic fish dipping sauce (page 28) or plum and peanut sauce (page 31), however, I really enjoy eating them with a Vietnamese chilli mayo (page 193).

Makes 6 rolls

6 sheets summer roll rice paper
30 viola flowers
120g smoked salmon
1 mango, as raw as possible, julienned
1 cucumber, julienned
1 large carrot, julienned
1 red bell pepper, julienned
12 large mint leaves
12 stems coriander
6 perilla leaves

Prawn and Pork Summer Rolls

Gỏi Cuốn Tôm Thịt Heo

This famous, deliciously healthy street-food dish is originally from Saigon; however, over the years, different regions have developed their own take on the ingredients. Definitely one of the beauties of this dish is that you are the creator of your summer rolls, so be as creative as you like.

Let's get started. Bring a saucepan of water to the boil, and add 2 pinches of salt and then the pork loin. Leave to cook for 15 minutes, then drain and plunge into iced water for 2–3 minutes. Drain again, pat dry with kitchen paper and slice very thinly.

Rinse the pan and fill with fresh water, adding 2 pinches of salt. Bring to the boil, add the prawns and cook for 2 minutes. Drain and plunge into iced water for 2–3 minutes. Drain again, remove the shells and then slice in half.

Cook the noodles in a saucepan of boiling water, following the timings on the packet. Drain, rinse in cold water, then drain again.

Let the rolling begin… Have a bowl of lukewarm water to wet the rice paper, and a chopping board or plate that is big enough to hold your rice paper for rolling.

Dunk the rice paper into the water very quickly and then lay flat on the board. Leave for about a minute, until almost dry before rolling. An easy way to set up is to work with 3 rolls at once. By the time you have laid the filling out on the third one, the first will be ready to roll.

Place your filling ingredients except the garlic chives in a line along the centre of the rice paper. Fold each side inwards towards the centre and then fold the paper from the bottom up, like an envelope. Place a stem of garlic chive across the envelope, with about 2.5cm sticking out of the roll. Press firmly using your fingertips and start folding. Be gentle but firm, controlling the movement and not allowing any of the filling to come out, making sure that the roll is tight. Continue to repeat the process until all your ingredients are used up.

You should have 8 rolls in total. Once made, you can store the rolls in an airtight container to keep them moist for up to 2–3 hours.

Serve with the fish dipping sauce.

Makes 8 rolls

6–8 sheets rice paper
Classic Fish Dipping Sauce
   (page 28), to serve

For the filling
4 pinches of salt
250g pork loin
250g raw king prawns
100g dried rice vermicelli noodles
½ head lettuce, washed and dried
2 carrots, finely sliced
100g coriander, washed
   and dried
100g mint, washed and dried
100g Thai basil, washed
   and dried
100g garlic chives

Vietnamese Crispy Pancakes with Pork and Prawns

Bánh Xèo Miền Nam

This is a national street food favourite! Pancake stands fill the markets of Vietnam with tantalising sounds and vibrant colours. Skilfully pan-fried over little gas burners, I would often find myself lost in admiration when stood next to a vendor, salivating at the thought of the first bite that was to follow.

This is one of those dishes where variations are found from region to region. The recipe here is the southern version; thin, crispy, large in size and eaten with plenty of fresh herbs! This is my grandpa's favourite meal and he's still the champion at rolling the biggest pancake lettuce wraps.

Prepare the pork belly. Bring a saucepan of water to the boil over a high heat. Add the pork belly, along with 2 pinches of salt. Lower the heat and simmer for 15 minutes, drain and plunge in iced water to cool. Slice thinly.

Rinse the pan and add fresh water. Bring the water to the boil over a high heat and add the prawns and 2 pinches of salt. Lower the heat and simmer for 4 minutes, then drain the prawns and plunge in iced water to cool. Remove the shells and devein.

Let's get started on the pancakes. Combine the flours, batter mix, coconut milk, salt, sugar, turmeric and water in a bowl and stir to form a smooth batter. Add the chopped spring onions and place in the fridge for 1 hour to set.

Heat 1 teaspoon of oil in a small non-stick pan over a high heat.

Add a few slices of pork belly and pieces of prawn, then ladle over just enough of the pancake batter to form a thin layer over the surface of the pan. Add a small handful of the vegetables, lower the heat, put the lid on and cook for 2½ minutes.

Remove the lid and maintain the low heat for a further 3½ minutes, until the pancake has that signature golden-yellow colour. Use a fish slice to fold the pancake, over the filling, into a half-moon. Take off the heat and it's ready to eat.

Repeat the process with the remaining batter and filling ingredients.

Have your platter of herbs and dipping sauce ready and let the rolling begin. The pancakes are best served wrapped in as many herbs as possible, then dipped in as much sauce as you can scoop… Well, that's the advice from my household anyway.

Makes 12 pancakes

225g rice flour
60g cornflour
8g tempura flour or batter mix
200ml coconut milk
large pinch of salt
3 teaspoons granulated sugar
1 teaspoon ground turmeric
750ml lukewarm water
6 spring onions, finely chopped
4 tablespoons vegetable oil

For the filling
400g pork belly
4 pinches of salt
400g raw prawns, shell on
2 pear squashes (optional), thinly sliced
50g bean sprouts
2 carrots, cut into fine matchsticks

To serve
20g mint leaves
20 Vietnamese mint
20g Thai basil
20g coriander
20g perilla leaves
3 baby gem lettuces, leaves separated
300ml Classic Fish Dipping Sauce (page 28)

Mini Prawn Pancakes

Bánh Khọt

A specialty street food dish from the central region of Vietnam, Đà Nẵng, that is almost too cute to eat. Almost.

For this dish, you will need to have a very specific frying pan. Don't worry, you don't have to go to Vietnam to get it, you can easily buy one online from the comfort of your lounge. The one that I use at the restaurant is an æbleskiver pan, although I'm sure there are others out there that have the same shape. You will need a lid for this recipe but don't worry if yours doesn't come with one as all you need to do is place over a small frying pan with sides steep enough to cover the bánh khọt without ruining the pancake toppings — works a treat.

Make the batter by putting all the ingredients into a bowl and mixing together well. Place in the fridge for at least 1 hour to give the batter a chance to rest. Remove from the fridge, and give the batter a stir to ensure an even consistency throughout.

Add 1 teaspoon of oil into each hole in your æbleskiver pan (see introduction) and place over a medium heat. Pour 1 tablespoon of the batter into each hole and allow it to sizzle away for 2 minutes.

Now, take a whole prawn and place it gently in the centre of each pancake, holding it upright for 10 seconds – this helps to position the prawn on the top of the bánh khọt. Repeat this for all the pancakes, then leave to cook for a further minute. Cover with the lid (or place over a small frying pan) and cook for a further 3 minutes at the same heat.

Take off the lid and continue to cook for a further 1–2 minutes. When you see a crispy rim around the edges of the pancakes, try moving the pancake a little. If it moves without sticking to the pan, it's ready. Take the pan off the heat and carefully use a palette knife to remove the pancakes.

Much like its big sister, bánh xèo, the best way to serve this is as a wrap to contain an abundance of fresh herbs. And, of course with the obligatory classic fish dipping sauce and, if you like, some pickled carrot and daikon.

This dish is best enjoyed if you don't count how many you've eaten. It's far too delicious to be worrying about things like that.

Makes 28 mini pancakes

120ml vegetable oil, for frying
300g raw king prawns, peeled
    and deveined

For the batter
225g rice flour
120g cornflour
200ml coconut milk
½ teaspoon salt
3 teaspoons granulated sugar
1 teaspoon turmeric
750ml lukewarm water
6 spring onions, finely chopped

To serve
20g mint leaves
20 Vietnamese mint
20g Thai basil
20g coriander
20g perilla leaves
3 baby gem lettuces, leaves
    separated
300ml Classic Fish Dipping
    Sauce (page 28)
200g Pickled Carrot and Daikon
    (page 23) (optional)

Beef Betel Leaf Skewers

Thịt Bò Nướng Lá Lốt

Betel leaves are heart-shaped shiny leaves that look deceptively normal; however, once they hit the grill, the air will be filled with a wonderful aroma and a sizzling sound that never fails to put a smile on your face. These little parcels are packed with flavour and are just perfect when drenched in classic fish dipping sauce.

Make the filling. In a mixing bowl, combine the minced beef with all the filling ingredients and mix together well. Cover and leave to marinate for 30 minutes in the fridge.

Let's get rolling… Place a betel leaf, shiny-side down, with the stem towards you on a board (2 leaves together, side by side, if they are small). Add approximately a tablespoon of the mixture, placing it on the leaf nearest to the stem. Place half a wedge of red onion on top, pressing it firmly onto the mix, then roll the leaf into a parcels starting from the stem.

Place the roll, seam-side down, onto the board so it stays in shape, then repeat this 3 more times. Thread all the rolls onto a skewer, making sure the tips are wedged together, especially the last one so it's secure when cooking.

Repeat the process for all 8 portions.

Cook the skewers on a ridged grill pan, hot plate or outdoor barbeque for best results. Allow 2 minutes per side, and no more than 5 minutes total for larger rolls.

Plate the skewers and sprinkle with crispy fried shallots and roasted peanuts. Traditionally, these are served with vermicelli noodles, a classic fish dipping sauce and a pile of fresh herbs.

Serves 6–8

32 medium–large betel leaves (4 leaves per portion), washed and dried on a cloth
1 red onion, sliced into small wedges
8 bamboo skewers

For the filling

500g minced beef
6 spring onions, white part only
3 lemongrass stalks, finely chopped
4 garlic cloves, finely chopped
1 tablespoon crushed black peppercorns
2 red chillies, finely chopped
1 teaspoon soy sauce
2 teaspoons fish sauce
1 tablespoon granulated sugar

To serve

1 tablespoon Crispy Fried Shallots (page 25)
1 tablespoon crushed Roasted Peanuts (page 26)
Classic Fish Dipping Sauce (page 28)

Pork and Mushroom Rice Rolls

Bánh Cuốn

A soft and delicately thin rice pancake, these rolls are filled with subtly seasoned pork mince, and are served with a variety of delicious toppings, giving amazing contrasts of temperature, flavour, texture and colour on every bite.

First make the batter by combining the ingredients in a bowl with 1 litre of water, stirring for 1–2 minutes until the mixture is smooth and the consistency of milk. Leave to rest for at least 1 hour.

To prepare the toppings, lightly oil a frying pan and set over a medium heat. Beat the eggs in a large bowl. Ladle just enough of the eggs to coat the bottom of the hot pan, tilting it to keep the layer thin. Allow to fry for 1 minute. Remove from the pan and place on a chopping board. When cool enough to handle, roll the egg sheet and slice very thinly. Repeat until all the eggs have been used.

Heat a frying pan over a medium–low heat. Add the Chinese sausage and fry for 30–40 seconds until starting to crisp up a little, then remove from the heat. If you like, fry the chả lụa as per the sausage above (not entirely necessary).

To make the filling, put the ingredients into a large bowl and knead together. The pork mince needs to be completely broken up so make sure to mix thoroughly.

Heat 2 tablespoons of vegetable oil in a frying pan over a medium heat until it reaches 160°C. An easy way to tell when the oil is ready is to place a wooden chopstick into it – when bubbles form on the surface of the oil it is ready. Add the shallots and the garlic, and stir-fry for 2 minutes until golden brown. Add the filling mixture and continue to stir-fry for a further 4 minutes, or until the meat is cooked through. Take the pan off the heat and set aside.

Line a large chopping board with foil and grease with 1 tablespoon of vegetable oil. Lightly brush a frying pan with vegetable oil and heat over a medium heat. Pour in a small ladle of the batter, tilting the pan in a circular motion to ensure the batter covers the entire base of the pan. You are aiming for a very thin layer, only a few millimetres thick. Cover with a lid and leave to cook over a medium heat for 45 seconds, until translucent. Remove the lid and carefully place on the greased chopping board. Now repeat the process to make a second pancake.

While the second pancake is cooking, spoon a generous tablespoon of the filling onto the pancake in a straight line just below the centre. Fold both sides of the pancake in first, then fold the bottom up, making an envelope-like shape, and then lightly roll upwards. This folding technique is very similar to the one used for spring or summer rolls but you need to be gentler with this as it's quite fragile. Arrange each roll on a plate and continue with the remaining pancakes and filling.

To serve, use a sharp pair of kitchen scissors to chop each roll into 4 pieces, then arrange on a serving plate. Repeat for all the rolls, stacking them into 2 layers. Scatter generous amounts of the sliced egg omelette, Chinese sausage and chả lụa on top of the rolls. Serve with the cucumbers, bean sprouts, a handful of each herb, a sprinkle of shallots and a generous amount of the dipping sauce.

Serves 8–10

vegetable oil
1 tablespoon finely diced
  Asian shallots
1 tablespoon finely diced garlic

For the batter
1 teaspoon vegetable oil
250g rice flour
250g tapioca flour

For the toppings
vegetable oil, for frying
10 eggs
10 Chinese sausages, cut
  into strips
400g chả lụa Vietnamese ham, cut
  into strips

For the filling
500g minced pork
2 carrots, finely diced
1 jicama, finely diced (or 50g water
  chestnuts)
100g wood ear mushrooms,
  soaked in warm water for 30
  minutes, drained and finely diced
1 teaspoon salt
3 teaspoons granulated sugar
1 teaspoon fish sauce
1 teaspoon soy sauce
2 tablespoons sesame oil
1 onion, finely diced

To serve
3 cucumbers, cut into matchsticks
500g bean sprouts, blanched in
  boiling water for 2 minutes
300g each mint, Thai basil and
  coriander, finely chopped
Classic Fish Dipping Sauce
  (page 28)
Crispy Fried Shallots (page 25)

Small
Plates

Vietnamese food isn't small! Typically meals are a spread of different dishes, designed to be shared, and encouraging you to interact with the food and each other. I remember, as a child, competing with my siblings to see who could make the biggest summer roll, cramming the most ingredients in. This is what Vietnamese food was made for! However, in contrast to the usual family-friendly feast, small plates, or nhậu, is actually a long-standing tradition in Vietnam. Literally translated, 'nhậu' means together and is made to be shared with friends. It is a Vietnamese-style of tapas that is eaten, usually only by men, in social settings, to accompany drinks.

The dishes involved in nhậu are often deemed not suitable for dinner, or for children, so are kept exclusively for these gatherings. They are seen to be more exotic and daring and they are designed to go well with the drink that usually accompanies nhậu sessions — beer! Often these dishes are overpowering in their flavours with salty and spicy seasoning dominating the palate. The main ingredient can often be more unusual meats, like frogs, eels, fermented pork or duck foetus', or more extravagant meats, like fillet steak, boar, quail, carpaccio or venison.

Customarily nhậu is a male pastime, as women don't drink in traditional Vietnamese culture. Whilst I am very respectful towards tradition, I do believe that there is a time for tradition to evolve and that these dishes should be shared and enjoyed by all. For me, the message that I am trying to get across in this book is that Vietnamese food is for everyone, everywhere. It is the most wonderful cuisine packed full of amazing flavours and my hope is that one day everybody will come to love it as I do.

Despite the fact that women typically would not eat these dishes, they are still generally the cooks behind them. Personally, I believe that chefs and home cooks alike are at their best when they're allowed to enjoy their food and are given the opportunity to experiment and really play with the recipes. To my mind, it is when crafting these wonderfully creative nhậu plates that the women really became chefs, experimenting with flavours and textures that were so different to the family meals they were used to making. The women who design and develop these dishes are truly amazing, and they, and their creations, genuinely inspire me everyday. These are dishes that elevate Vietnamese food to something ground breaking and really showcase the best of what our cuisine has to offer.

I'm going to show you how to make a few small plates in this chapter that are accessible to everyone whilst still being super flavoursome. These are nonetheless dishes that would grace any nhậu table and all of them are regularly eaten as such up and down the country… Although I think we'll leave the duck foetus for another book!

Salt and Pepper King Prawns

Tôm Rang Muối Tiêu

Only 20 minutes to make, these delicately seasoned king prawns are a beautifully light and delicious snack.

Heat the vegetable oil in a deep-fat fryer, or large frying pan over a medium heat, until it reaches 160°C. An easy way to tell when the oil is ready is to place a wooden chopstick into it – when bubbles form on the surface of the oil it is ready.

Thinly coat the prawns in cornflour. Carefully add to the hot oil and deep-fry for 3 minutes until golden. Remove with a slotted spoon and drain on kitchen paper.

In a small bowl, combine the salt, sugar and peppercorns then set aside for later.

In a frying pan, over a medium heat, add the sesame oil. Add the garlic, chillies, spring onions, shallots, lemongrass and ginger. Evenly distribute the ingredients in the pan, then add the prawns.

Sprinkle the salt, sugar and peppercorn mix evenly over the prawns and toss until they are evenly covered in the seasoning.

Arrange the prawns on a plate, squeeze a wedge of lime on top and it's ready to eat.

Serves 2–3 as part of a meal of many sharing dishes

500ml vegetable oil
6 raw king prawns, deveined, tail and head on
cornflour, for dusting
2 teaspoons sea salt
2 teaspoons granulated sugar
2 teaspoons crushed black peppercorns
4 tablespoons sesame oil
1 tablespoon finely chopped garlic
1 tablespoon finely chopped red chillies
6 spring onions, cut into 5cm pieces
8 Asian shallots, thinly sliced
2 stems lemongrass, crushed and chopped into 4cm long pieces
20g ginger, peeled and julienned
lime wedge, to serve

Grilled Giant Tiger Prawns in Honey

I'm very lucky and am able to source incredible giant prawns, but if you can't, just use what you can find. Any prawns in this delicious marinade are perfect with a rice or salad dish, on top of a delicious noodle bowl or simply served as one of several dishes in a Vietnamese-style family meal. However you chose to serve them, these sweet, juicy prawns will be a great addition to your table.

Place all the marinade ingredients into a shallow bowl and mix together thoroughly.

Add the prawns to the bowl and rub the marinade in well, paying extra attention to the cut on the prawn where you deveined them.

Leave in the fridge to marinate for a minimum of 30 minutes, or for the perfect flavour, I'd recommend leaving them for 3 hours.

Preheat the oven to 180°C/160°C Fan/Gas Mark 4.

Place the prawns on a baking tray and bake for 12–15 minutes, turning them halfway through cooking. They should be a deep red-pink colour when done. If you aren't able to source giant prawns then you may only need as little cooking time as 5 minutes, so keep an eye on them.

Once out of the oven they are ready to eat! I love to drizzle them with the amazing chilli and lemongrass marinade (page 21), to give it that extra kick on the bite that I can't get enough of, or you can serve with a simple fish sauce and chilli dip.

Serves 2

2 giant tiger prawns, 350g each, deveined with head and shell on

For the marinade
4 large garlic cloves, finely diced
1 teaspoon soy sauce
1 teaspoon fish sauce
3 teaspoons honey
½ fresh lime, juiced
2 tablespoons sesame oil

Mussels with Chilli, Ginger and Lemongrass

Chẽm Chép Xào Sả Ớt Và Gừng

An uncomplicated, elegant dish that simply relies on a mild kick of chilli, ginger and lemongrass to tantalise your taste buds. The perfect sharing dish for a light dinner.

Wash the mussels in cold water and scrub them thoroughly. Remove the 'hairy beards'. Soak the mussels in a large bowl filled with plenty of cold water for 1 hour. Soaking the mussels helps to extract any excess dirt and sand that can ruin the dish. Throw out any mussels with broken shells or any that do not close when given a firm tap.

Heat the oil in a saucepan over a medium heat until it reaches 160°C. An easy way to tell when the oil is ready is to place a wooden chopstick into it – when bubbles form on the surface of the oil it is ready. Add the garlic, lemongrass and ginger, and fry for 3 minutes, until slightly golden brown in colour. Stir in the remaining ingredients, except for the spring onion oil and dipping sauce, then stir-fry for a few seconds and throw in the mussels. Cover with the lid and cook for 5 minutes, over a medium heat, until the mussels have opened. Throw out any mussels that have not opened before serving.

Garnish with a drizzle of spring onion oil, and serve alongside a classic fish dipping sauce and lime wedges. This dish is also great as a starter or snack if served alongside salt, pepper and lime dip (page 27).

Serves 4

1kg mussels
3 tablespoons vegetable oil
20g garlic cloves, peeled and
   finely diced
4 lemongrass stalks, finely sliced
200g ginger, cut into fine
   matchsticks
2 tablespoons fish sauce
2 tablespoons rice wine
2 teaspoons granulated sugar
200g red chillies, cut into
   fine matchsticks
200g Asian shallots, thinly sliced
200ml coconut water

To serve
Spring Onion Oil (page 22)
Classic Fish Dipping Sauce
   (page 28)
lime wedges

Lemongrass Clams

Nghêu Xào Sả

I love the simplicity of a great seafood dish and this is one of my favourites. Infusing the ginger, chilli and lemongrass is quick and easy, yet so effective. Eating the clams is fabulous of course, but for me, drinking that sweet broth at the end is just the best!

Rinse the clams in cold water, brush clean the shells thoroughly, then soak them for 1 hour in a large bowl of fresh cold water, adding 1 tablespoon of salt. Make sure the water covers the clams well – this step helps to take away any excess sand or grit from the clams. Throw out any clams with broken shells or any that do not close when given a firm tap.

Heat the oil in a saucepan over a medium heat. Add the garlic, red onions, chillies, lemongrass and ginger, and sauté for 2 minutes. Drain the clams and add to the pan along with the lime juice, fish sauce, sugar and rice wine. Cover the pan with a lid and continue to cook for 2 minutes. Check that all the clams have opened up, then turn off the heat immediately and serve. Discard the whole lemongrass stalks.

Transfer to a serving bowl, drizzle over the annatto seed oil, and garnish with Thai basil, coriander leaves and spring onions, if using. Now tuck in!

Serves 2

1kg clams
1 tablespoon salt, for cleaning
   clams
2 tablespoons vegetable oil
2 tablespoons finely diced garlic
2 tablespoons finely diced
   red onions
2 tablespoons finely diced
   red chillies
4 lemongrass stalks, 1 stalk finely
   chopped and 3 stalks halved
   then crushed
200g ginger, cut into
   fine matchsticks
3 tablespoons lime juice
1 tablespoon fish sauce
1 tablespoon granulated sugar
200ml rice wine
1 teaspoon Annatto Seed Oil
   (page 22)

To serve (optional)
100g Thai basil leaves
100g coriander leaves
5 spring onions, finely chopped

Chargrilled Chilli Squid

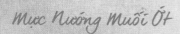

A Vietnamese night-market staple and a favourite of the traditional nhậu gatherings. Sliced into bite-sized pieces this is the perfect snack when you have a drink in your other hand!

First, prepare the squid if you've bought it whole. Spread the squid out on a chopping board and reach up inside the cavity to remove all the internal organs including the pen, which looks like a plastic feather, and throw these away.

Cut the tentacles away from the body just below the eyes, clean and set aside. Give the squid a good pull at the base so that the beak pops out and then remove. Cut or pull the purple skin from the squid to leave just the white meat. Cut the fins from the squid and discard.

Now, thoroughly rinse the squid inside and out to get ride of excess sand or grit.

Mix the ingredients for the marinade together in a small bowl and thoroughly rub this into the squid and the tentacles. Leave to marinate for 3 hours in the fridge.

In a small bowl, combine the ingredients for the dipping sauce. Set aside.

Remove the squid and tentacles from the marinade. Preheat a ridged grill pan over a medium heat. When hot, add the squid and tentacles and cook for 2 minutes and then turn over to cook for a further 2 minutes. You want to get those lovely black grill lines across the flesh. Push the squid down with the back of a fish slice for a few seconds to finish off. Take off the heat and serve with the salt, pepper and lime dip. Easy and delicious!

Serves 4 as part of a meal of many sharing dishes

600–700g whole squid or
　prepared squid pieces
Salt, Pepper and Lime Dip
　(page 27), to serve

For the marinade
2 teaspoons Annatto Seed Oil
　(page 22)
1 tablespoon finely chopped
　red chillies
1 tablespoon fish sauce
1 teaspoon salt

Grilled Lemongrass Beef Skewers

Thịt Bò Nướng Sả

This dish may only be in the oven for 20 minutes but if you're anything like me the smell of it cooking will make you so hungry it will be impossible not to sneak a taste early. On the positive side, the aroma of this fragrant dish lingers around your kitchen, so once you've eaten and your hunger is sated you can enjoy it for a while longer. This is one of my favourite show-off dishes when cooking for family and friends. Very little effort is involved yet it looks impressive and tastes so good.

Place the beef in the freezer for about 30 minutes (this will make it easier to slice). Remove from the freezer and slice thinly against the grain into long strips. Aim for pieces approximately 2.5cm high × 10cm long.

Combine the beef strips along with all the ingredients for the marinade in a bowl. Be as gentle as possible while mixing; the beef strips are quite delicate and the key to the success of this dish is being able to keep the strips long and intact. Cover and allow to marinate in the fridge, preferably overnight for perfect results but for at least 3 hours. Take the beef out of the fridge 30–45 minutes before cooking to bring it up to room temperature.

To make the spring onion oil, heat the oil in a saucepan over a medium heat until it reaches 160°C. An easy way to tell when the oil is ready is to place a wooden chopstick into it – when bubbles form on the surface of the oil it is ready. Add the salt and spring onions, then immediately take the pan off the heat and leave to cool on the side.

To make the glaze, combine all the ingredients well in a bowl. Set aside.

Preheat the oven to 180°C/160°C Fan/Gas Mark 4.

For each lemongrass stalk, take 2–3 strips of beef and wrap them around the lemongrass stalk, with each successive strip overlapping the last a little, making sure that the stalk is covered about two-thirds by the beef. Overlapping the meat is a must as it creates layers that helps to keep all the delicious flavours of the marinade in, as well making it much meatier and juicier to the bite. When you've completed your wrapping, place the skewers on a baking tray so the ends of the beef strips face down. Repeat with the remaining beef and lemongrass stalks.

Brush the skewers all over with the honeyed glaze. Arrange on a baking tray lined with foil. Cook in the oven for 10 minutes, turn the skewers, brush on some more of the glaze and cook for a further 10 minutes. Remove from the oven, arrange on a serving plate, then sprinkle with the peanuts and drizzle with the spring onion oil. These can be served as a starter or snack, or as part of a sharing platter. Alternatively, serve with cooked rice noodles and fresh herbs and a classic fish dipping sauce (page 28) or – my personal favourite – as a filling for summer rolls.

Makes 16

500g beef topside
16 lemongrass stalks
Roasted Peanuts (page 26),
  to serve

For the marinade
2 tablespoons finely diced red
  chillies
2 tablespoons finely diced garlic
2 tablespoons finely diced
  lemongrass stalks
2 tablespoons finely diced spring
  onions, white parts
2 tablespoons fish sauce
1 tablespoon soy sauce
pinch of salt
3 tablespoons granulated sugar
4 tablespoons sesame oil

For the spring onion oil
120ml vegetable oil
1 teaspoon salt
6 spring onions, thinly sliced

For the honeyed glaze
75g honey
75ml Annatto Seed Oil (page 22)
3 tablespoons soy sauce

Lemongrass and Chilli Pork Ribs and Chicken Wings

Sườn Heo Và Cánh Gà Nướng Sả Ớt

Come rain or shine, I'm never one to shy away from a good Vietnamese barbeque! This dish is perfect for those chilled and relaxed kind of gatherings where there's no need for chairs and fingers are used instead of cutlery. It's an easy dish to make that will take your barbeque game to the next level! Go on, you know it's a must!

In a bowl, combine all the ingredients for the marinade and mix well. Pour half the mixture into a separate bowl and add the chicken wings. Thoroughly massage the marinade into the chicken wings and leave to marinate in the fridge for at least 3 hours, or ideally overnight. Repeat the process with the remaining marinade and the pork ribs.

Take the meat out of the fridge at least 30 minutes before cooking to allow it to come to room temperature.

Here are a few options for how to cook the chicken wings and pork ribs.

Sunny day option: barbeque
To cook the chicken on the barbeque, grill for 20–25 minutes, turning halfway through the cooking time. The wings are cooked when the flesh is no longer pink in the middle.

To cook the pork ribs on the, grill for 25–30 minutes, turning often until nicely browned.

Rainy day option: oven roasted
For the chicken, preheat the oven to 180°C/160°C Fan/Gas Mark 4.

Arrange the chicken wings on a baking tray lined with foil, leaving the marinade behind and setting it aside for later. Roast for 40 minutes, turning halfway through the cooking time. Brush over the reserved marinade and continue to roast for a further 10 minutes.

For the pork ribs, preheat the oven to 200°C/180°C Fan/Gas Mark 6.

Arrange the ribs on a baking tray and brush on some of the marinade, leaving a little for later. Roast for 50 minutes, turning the ribs after 25 minutes. Brush over the reserved marinade and continue to cook for a further 10 minutes.

Scatter with the chillies and spring onions and serve alongside the pineapple fish dipping sauce. You could serve this with rice or vermicelli noodles and a side salad. Alternatively, a good crusty baguette is always a crowd-pleaser.

Serves 4

1kg chicken wings, any extra fatty skin removed
1kg pork ribs, washed and cut into single ribs

For the marinade
8 lemongrass stalks, crushed and finely diced
12 Asian shallots, finely diced
4 bird's eye chillies, finely diced
3 tablespoons fish sauce
1 tablespoon soy sauce
3 tablespoons granulated sugar
1 tablespoon honey
1 tablespoon crushed black peppercorns
90ml sesame oil

To serve
2 or 3 red chillies, sliced lengthways
100g spring onions, finely sliced on the diagonal
Pineapple Fish Sauce (page 29)

Shaking Beef

Bò Lúc Lắc

Here, beef fillet is tossed in black
peppercorns, flash-seared rare and served
with a zingy watercress and red onion salad.
(The image shows an unadulterated bowl of
the delicious beef, but it's amazing served
with all the extras, so follow the recipe to
get the best flavours.)

  Bò lúc lắc is irresistible. The flavours are
intensely delicious and the charred exterior
of the beef contrasts nicely with the rare,
melt-in-the-mouth interior. The accompanying
pickled onions offer a beautiful tangy kick
to the whole dish. And the classic dipping
sauce of salt, crushed black peppercorns
and a generous squeeze of fresh lime is
simple yet adds so much depth and flavour.
I would confidently say that any one of these
components would have any Vietnamese person
salivating, let alone all of them combined
together on one plate.

  Mummy Pham would often make bò lúc lắc for
dad and his friends as a tapas-style snack
to accompany beer. Oh, the number of times
I wished I could sneak up to the table with
my chopsticks…

continued on page 156...

Shaking Beef...

Put the beef and all of the ingredients for the marinade in a bowl. Mix well and place in the fridge for 3 hours to allow the marinade to fully flavour the beef. Remove the beef from the fridge about 30 minutes before cooking to bring it back up to room temperature.

To make the dipping sauce, combine the salt and pepper in a small bowl, squeeze over the lime and mix briefly. It should all mix together nicely leaving a lovely textured dip.

In a small bowl, make a vinaigrette by combining the lime juice, sugar, garlic, chilli and fish sauce. Stir until the sugar has completely dissolved. Add the red onions and use your fingers to lightly toss together. Be careful not to bruise the onions. Set aside for the onions to pickle.

Heat 1 tablespoon of oil in a frying pan over a medium heat. When the oil is hot, add the spring onions and sauté for 1 minute. Immediately remove the pan from the heat – the spring onions should still be green in colour and have some bite. Transfer to a small bowl and set aside.

Wipe the pan clean with paper towels, add the remaining 2 tablespoons of oil to the pan and set over a high heat until it reaches 190°C. An easy way to tell when the oil is ready is to place a wooden chopstick into it – when lots of bubbles form on the surface of the oil it is ready. Add the beef and its marinade and spread out evenly in the pan. Depending on how large your pan is, you may want to do this in batches to prevent overcrowding the meat. Sear the beef for 30 seconds, then turn the pieces over and sear the other side for a further 30 seconds.

Now, lift the pan off the stovetop and toss the beef vigorously. This step is how the dish got its name, so feel free to go to town on your 'shaking'! If you do this right you can expect lots of flames and drama. Shake the pan for 30 seconds, over a high heat at all times. Never take your eyes off the meat – don't allow it to burn. Add the spring onions, and continue shaking for a further 15 seconds. The beef should be nicely charred on the outside and rare in the middle.

Scatter the watercress over a large serving plate. By now, the red onion pickle should now be ready, so scatter the pickle over the watercress, and arrange the beef on top.

Garnish the dish with crispy fried shallots and you're good to go. This is also great served with other small plates but can be enjoyed on its own, and as a main meal, with freshly steamed rice.

Serves 4 as part of a meal of many sharing dishes

500g beef fillet, cut into
   2.5cm dice
3 tablespoons vegetable oil
10 spring onions, sliced
   diagonally into 5cm pieces

For the beef marinade
4 tablespoons sesame oil
2 tablespoons finely diced garlic
2 tablespoons finely diced
   red chillies
2 tablespoons black peppercorns
2 tablespoons granulated sugar
1 tablespoon fish sauce
1 tablespoon soy sauce
1 tablespoon rice wine
1 teaspoon oyster sauce

For the dipping sauce
1 teaspoon salt
2 teaspoons crushed black
   peppercorns
juice of 1 lime

For the pickled onions
juice of 2 limes
4 tablespoons granulated sugar
1 teaspoon finely chopped garlic
1 teaspoon finely chopped red
   chilli
1 tablespoon fish sauce
2 red onions, cut into fine
   matchsticks

To serve
200g watercress
1 tablespoon Crispy Fried
   Shallots (page 25)

Crispy Fish Sauce Chicken Wings

Cánh Gà Chiên Nước Mắm

Don't be put off by the name — even the fish sauce deniers out there will be truly addicted to this one. Packed with flavour and overwhelmingly moreish. I hope you have your beer ready!

Using a sharp knife, cut each chicken wing into 3 pieces. Put the drumsticks and the flat pieces to one side and throw the wingtips away.

In a bowl, combine the chicken and all of the ingredients for the marinade, then mix well. Leave to marinate in the fridge for at least 3 hours, or ideally overnight.

Line a tray with paper towels. Heat the oil in a frying pan over a medium heat until it reaches 160°C. An easy way to tell when the oil is ready is to place a wooden chopstick into it – when bubbles form on the surface of the oil it is ready.

Remove the chicken from the marinade, reserving the marinade for later. Use a paper towel to wipe away any excess marinade from the chicken pieces. Place the cornflour in a shallow bowl. Dip the chicken pieces into the cornflour, coating them all over, then carefully drop into the hot oil. Deep-fry for 3–5 minutes, until perfectly golden and cooked through. Depending on the size of your pan you may wish to deep-fry the chicken in batches.

Remove the chicken from the pan and drain on the lined tray. Leave to cool while you get on with the glaze.

Pour all the leftover marinade into a frying pan and bring to the boil over a medium heat. Cook for 3–4 minutes, until the mixture appears caramelised and syrupy. Add the chicken pieces, tossing to coat them well in the sticky glaze. Add the spring onions and chillies, then take the pan off the heat immediately. Keep tossing, as the residual heat in the pan will wilt the spring onions a little.

Serve the chicken with fish sauce mixed with fresh chillies. Yes, more chillies and more fish sauce…

These make a great snack or starter in their own right. For a perfect yet simple combo, serve with fluffy and freshly cooked rice.

Serves 3–4

1kg chicken wings
1 litre vegetable oil
70g cornflour
6 spring onions, thinly sliced
3 red chillies, thinly sliced diagonally

For the marinade

3 tablespoons sesame oil
1 teaspoon salt
75ml fish sauce
80g granulated sugar
2 tablespoons finely diced garlic
2 tablespoons finely diced ginger

To serve

20ml fish sauce
2 red chillies, sliced
Crispy Fried Shallots (page 25)
Crispy Garlic (page 26)

Colours
of Vietnam

Colours of Vietnam

Typically you would think that stir-fries and salads should be amongst the easiest recipes in this book, and in a way you'd be right. It is very easy to knock together a passable dish; however, I find there is a huge imbalance between the perception and what is actually needed to make these dishes absolutely perfect. Sometimes the quickest dishes are the easiest to mess up! The fewer the steps and ingredients, the bigger the difference that over or undercooking one will make. In my opinion it is in the simplest dishes that you can tell the very best cooks, so when you get them right, they are plates worth showing off!

So, a small piece of advice: make sure you prep well and leave plenty of time to cook the recipes in this chapter. Make them perfect!

My mum has such high standards. To please her, every ingredient that goes into these recipes needs to be perfectly chopped to maximise texture, and marinated exactly to maximise flavour. As frustrating as I found this as a teenager, as is so often the case, I have found myself turning into my mother and have started insisting on it too. Now whilst I hate to do anything for the sake of it, I can genuinely see her point that if you can do something, however small, to make the dish better, then you absolutely should. No dish should ever leave your kitchen unless it's perfect.

As you can tell, we both have high expectations and to make these recipes to our standard means investing a good amount of prep-time in them. So, my top tip is always to prep, prep, prep! Follow my mum's example and take the time to prepare the ingredients in the ways that I suggest over the following pages. It is so important and if you do it properly, taking due time and care, these dishes will be elevated beyond your expectations. I also recommend that you use the very best ingredients you can find. They should be as fresh as you can get them and organic if you can stretch to it. Obviously this applies to all of the recipes in the book, but it's harder to hide poor ingredients when making such simple dishes.

One of the great things about stir-fries and salads is that they are incredibly flexible. In Vietnam, the fresh ingredients that we'd use were grown on the family farm, so we always had an abundance of fresh vegetables and herbs for these dishes. One of the herbs my grandma used to grow was water spinach. Ordinarily in Vietnam this is not an ingredient to add to a stir-fry and in fact, is generally only grown to feed to the pigs. However, as well as being the pigs' favourite, it was also mine! So she would always keep some aside to stir-fry for me. As you can imagine this was considered hilarious by my family and my nickname soon became 'mini-pig'; apparently the uglier the nickname, the more love there is behind it. At least that's what they told me at the time.

Vietnamese food is all about contrasting textures and flavours and so I've tried to show you how to create intricate layers of them in these recipes. They are made by building up simple contrasts, like hot and cold, crunchy and tender, or sweet and sour. They are great fun to play with and I would encourage you to try out some of your own. These recipes are for authentic dishes made everyday in Vietnam. Each province of the country has its own variations and these are from my home region of the Mekong Delta. However, I definitely suggest that you follow my grandma's lead and experiment with them by adding extra items of your own. Just make sure they complement the other ingredients you are using. Remember, each and every addition should add a new dimension to the dish: a new flavour or texture.

As an added bonus to tasting amazing, Vietnamese salads and stir-fries are really good for you! They are packed full of greens and herbs and naturally gluten and dairy-free. Each of the recipes in this chapter is a riot of colour too! I've always said that Vietnamese food feeds your eyes before you even start to eat, as it looks so scrumptious and beautiful. This is definitely the case with these recipes, as you will see. So vibrantly colourful, healthy and, most importantly, delicious.

Each of these recipes showcases important techniques of Vietnamese cooking and my absolute favourite ingredients. To me, they are a real taste of home and my unsung heroes of Vietnamese food. I hope you love them!

Morning Glory Stir-fry

Rau Muống Xào Tỏi

When I was growing up this was my mother's go-to dish when she was in a fight against time with the daily errands and still wanted to squeeze in time to prepare a full Vietnamese family meal for when dad got home from a long day's work. So, pull this one from your bag when you need a dish that takes minutes to make, but tastes like it took hours!

Heat the sesame oil in a frying pan over a medium heat. When the oil is hot, add the garlic and stir-fry for 1 minute, or until golden. Add the morning glory, fish sauce and the salt. Stir-fry for a few seconds, then add the sugar. Keep tossing from this point onwards to make sure that everything is mixed evenly and the sugar doesn't burn or caramelise. After 2 minutes, take the pan off the heat and plate up. For the finishing touch, garnish with the crispy fried shallots, crispy garlic, sliced lemongrass and chillies.

Traditionally, this would be served with other dishes, and rice, and always with a little dish of soy sauce with some sliced chilli in. However, I would be perfectly happy serving this as a light and healthy lunch by itself.

Serves 4 as part of a meal of many sharing dishes

3 tablespoons sesame oil
2 tablespoons finely diced garlic
500g morning glory, roughly chopped
1 tablespoon fish sauce
pinch of salt
1 tablespoon granulated sugar

To serve
Crispy Fried Shallots (page 25)
Crispy Garlic (page 26)
1 lemongrass stalk, sliced
2 red chillies, sliced lengthways

Tofu and Shiitake Dry Noodle Bowl

Bún Xào Tàu Hũ Nấm Đông Cô

A beautiful and super-healthy vegan dish, that categorically doesn't compromise on flavour!

Prepare the vermicelli noodles according to the packet instructions. Set aside.

Heat the oil in a large frying pan over a medium heat. Add the garlic, chilli and lemongrass, then stir-fry until the garlic turns light brown in colour. Add the carrots and continue to stir-fry for a further minute. Now add the pear squash, red onions and shiitake mushrooms, and stir-fry for a further 2 minutes.

Add the tofu, soy sauce, sugar and mushroom oyster sauce, then stir-fry for 2 more minutes. For a final touch, sprinkle over the spring onions and black peppercorns, then toss well. It's now ready to portion into your serving bowls.

To top each serving bowl, add a small handful of bean sprouts, then a portion of the noodles. Add the tofu stir-fry on top, pour over 3–4 tablespoons of vegan soy dipping sauce and then finally garnish with the herbs.

Serves 6

400g packet dried vermicelli noodles

3 tablespoons vegetable oil

1 tablespoon finely chopped garlic

1 tablespoon finely chopped red chilli

1 tablespoon finely chopped lemongrass

2 large carrots, cut into fine matchsticks

1 pear squash, peeled and cut into fine matchsticks

1 red onion, finely sliced

10 Soy-braised Shiitake Mushrooms, very thinly sliced (page 24)

400g Deep-fried Tofu (page 25), cut into 1cm strips

1 tablespoon soy sauce

1 tablespoon granulated sugar

1 tablespoon mushroom oyster sauce

3 spring onions, finely chopped

1 teaspoon crushed black peppercorns

To serve
200g bean sprouts

270ml Vegan Soy Dipping Sauce (page 30)

100g coriander, chopped

100g Thai basil leaves

100g mint leaves

Papaya and Tamarind Tiger Prawns

Gỏi Đu Đủ Tôm Nước Mắm Me

This dish makes a great starter or light lunch. Alternatively, you can serve it as part of a larger Vietnamese sharing meal.

Season the prawns with the salt and crushed black peppercorns.

Melt the butter in a frying pan over a medium–high heat. Arrange the prawns in the pan and fry for 2 minutes, on each side, or until golden. Remove the prawns from the pan.

In a large bowl, combine the remaining ingredients. Add the prawns to the bowl and toss everything together.

Plate up, sprinkle with the garnishes and tuck in.

Serves 2

12 raw tiger prawns, peeled, heads removed, deveined and patted dry with paper towels
¼ teaspoon salt
¼ teaspoon crushed black peppercorns
1 teaspoon butter
1 papaya (approximately 750g), cut into 5cm matchsticks
1 large daikon, cut into fine matchsticks 5cm in length
1 cucumber, seeds removed and cut into fine matchsticks 5cm in length
10g Thai basil, finely chopped
10g mint, finely chopped
10g Vietnamese mint, finely chopped
10g coriander, finely chopped
150ml Tamarind Fish Sauce (page 29)

To serve
1 tablespoon Roasted Peanuts (page 26)
1 tablespoon Crispy Fried Shallots (page 25)
1 teaspoon Crispy Garlic (page 26)

Squash and Prawn Stir-fry

Su Su Xào Tôm

It looks like a fruit, tastes like a vegetable and the name is confusing, 'pear squash' — clearly it can't make up its mind. Either way, it tastes amazing with prawns, so who cares about its identity crisis.

In a bowl, combine the prawns and the ingredients for the marinade, and mix together well. Leave to marinate at room temperature for 30 minutes.

Heat 3 tablespoons of oil in a frying pan over a medium heat until it reaches 160°C. An easy way to tell when the oil is ready is to place a wooden chopstick into it – when bubbles form on the surface of the oil it is ready.

Throw in the prawns and stir-fry for 2 minutes. The sizzle they make as they hit the pan has to be one of my favourite sounds in the world. Keep the prawns moving constantly using your spatula or chopsticks to keep the prawns from sticking together. Take the pan off the heat and transfer the prawns to a bowl to set aside.

Return the pan to the heat and add the remaining 3 tablespoons of oil. When hot, add the garlic and ginger, and stir-fry for about 20 seconds until golden. Next, add the pear squash, rice wine, sugar and soy sauce. Continue to stir-fry for 2 minutes, then return the prawns to the pan with all their wonderful marinade sauce. Toss for a further minute, and it's ready.

Garnish with the spring onions. This is great served with jasmine rice, and a simple dipping sauce of fish sauce and sliced red chillies served on the side would also be delicious.

Serves 2–3 as part of a meal of many sharing dishes

16 raw prawns, peeled and deveined, leaving the tails on
6 tablespoons vegetable oil
1 tablespoon minced garlic
1 tablespoon minced ginger
2 pear squash, peeled, seeds removed and cut into fine matchsticks
2 tablespoons rice wine
1 tablespoon granulated sugar
1 tablespoon soy sauce
2 spring onions, thinly sliced diagonally, to serve

For the marinade
1 teaspoon cornflour
1 tablespoon fish sauce
1 tablespoon Annatto Seed Oil (page 22)
pinch of salt

Sweet and Sour Squid Stir-fry

Mực Sao Chua Ngọt

Growing up I would often have this dish with vermicelli rice noodles instead of the traditional jasmine rice, definitely a Mummy Pham twist and one I still love. When serving, as here, with rice, I would always suggest drizzling a bit of classic fish dipping sauce (page 28), into the bowl.

Heat 3 tablespoons of oil in a frying pan over a high heat until it reaches 190°C. An easy way to tell when the oil is ready is to place a wooden chopstick into it – when bubbles form on the surface of the oil it is ready.

Add the squid along with all the seasoning ingredients and stir-fry for 2 minutes. Remove from the pan and set aside in a bowl.

Add the remaining oil to the pan and place over a high heat. Add the pineapple and tomatoes and stir-fry for 1 minute. Add the spring onions, onion, shallot, cucumber and celery, and stir-fry for a further minute. Lastly return the squid to the pan along with all the flavoursome oil in the bowl. Stir-fry for a further minute and it's ready to serve.

Transfer to a large plate, top with some of the garnishes (keeping the rest aside for people to add as they like). This is great served with steamed jasmine rice and a bowl of soy sauce with some sliced chilli.

Serves 2

6 tablespoons vegetable oil
300g prepared squid, lightly scored and cut into 5cm pieces
½ pineapple, peeled, eyes removed and cut into small chunks
12 cherry tomatoes
4 spring onions, chopped into 3cm lengths
1 onion, cut into 2cm wedges and halved
4 red shallots, cut into halves
1 cucumber, halved, seeds removed and sliced diagonally into 1cm thick pieces
200g Chinese celery, sliced diagonally

For the seasoning
1 tablespoon finely diced garlic
1 tablespoon fish sauce
1 tablespoon soy sauce
2 tablespoons rice wine
2 tablespoons granulated sugar
½ teaspoon salt
juice of ½ lime
1 teaspoon black peppercorns

To serve (optional)
3 red chillies, thinly sliced diagonally
1 tablespoon Crispy Fried Shallots (page 25)
2 spring onions, thinly sliced diagonally
small handful of coriander, roughly chopped
small handful of Thai basil leaves

Chicken and Mango Salad

Gỏi Gà Trộn Xoà

This is a great dish served on its own as a main course or as a side as part of a shared family meal. Traditionally, it is eaten with steamed rice or rice porridge cháo or congee.

Make the dressing. In a saucepan, over a medium heat, add fish sauce, lime juice, sugar and 100ml of water. Stir until the sugar is dissolved and take the pan off the heat before boiling point. Allow the dressing to completely cool down, then add the garlic and chillies. If they float on the surface, it's a success. (If they sink to the bottom, the sauce was still too warm.)

Store in a tightly sealed jar and refrigerate for up to 5 days.

Preheat the oven to 170°C/150°C Fan/Gas Mark 3.

Grease a roasting dish with butter. Rub the sesame oil evenly over the chicken breasts and place in the dish. Cover the dish with baking paper. Place in the oven for 25–30 minutes, depending on the size of the chicken breasts, until cooked through and golden. Leave to cool, then hand tear into strips. Set aside.

Start prepping the salad. Peel the mango and thinly slice into julienned strips.

In a mixing bowl, combine the mangoes, chicken, green herbs and spring onions, and finish with the fish sauce dressing. Lightly toss, then plate.

Scatter the final touches of chilli, crispy fried shallots, crispy garlic and crushed peanuts on top.

Serves 2, or 3–4 as part of a meal of many sharing dishes

butter, for greasing
2 tablespoons sesame oil
300g boneless chicken breasts
2 unripe (green) mangoes
  (180–200g each)
small handful of mint leaves,
  chopped
small handful of coriander,
  chopped
2 spring onions, chopped
5–6 tablespoons Fish Sauce and
  Lime Salad Dressing (page 28),
  to taste

For the dressing
3 tablespoons fish sauce
juice of 1 lime
3 tablespoons granulated sugar
3 garlic cloves, finely chopped
2 bird's eye chillies, finely
  chopped

To serve
1 red chilli, thinly sliced into
  slanted hoops
1 teaspoon Crispy Fried Shallots
  (page 25)
1 teaspoon Crispy Garlic
  (page 26)
1 tablespoon crushed Roasted
  Peanuts (page 26)

Aromatic Duck, Sweet Pea and Tamarind Salad

Gỏi Vịt Đọt Đậu Nước Mắm Me

Eastern flavours combine beautifully here with Western cooking techniques. To this day, my mum still shakes her head at the sight of rare meat dishes, ceviche or runny eggs leaving my kitchen. I sometimes wonder if this would have been the case for me too had I not moved to England so young. I hope that she is secretly impressed though; I *have* noticed a telling glint in her eye on occasion.

Being a Vietnamese mummy, she definitely reveals a suspicion of unfamiliarity when my cooking strays from the traditional. It's strange to me because she makes the most amazing Vietnamese beef carpaccio for dad and his friends, and yet she won't eat it herself or consider playing with the technique on other meats or other dishes. I'd hate to see her reaction if I made a steak tartare. I suspect I'd be looking for the nearest fire escape!

First, make the dressing. In a small bowl, combine the tamarind paste with the hot water. Strain and reserve the liquid.

Heat 20ml of water in a saucepan, add the sugar, and stir until it dissolves. Take the pan off the heat and leave the mixture to cool for 20 minutes. Add the fish sauce, tamarind liquid, chillies and garlic to the sugar water, and mix together.

Next, blitz all the spices in a spice grinder and put into a small dish.

Pat the duck breasts dry with paper towels. Using a sharp knife, score the skin being careful to cut only through the skin and fat and not into the flesh. Season each duck breast all over with a pinch each of salt and the spice mix.

Preheat your oven to 200°C/180°C Fan/Gas Mark 6.

Place a duck breast, skin-side down, in a non-stick frying pan. Place over a medium heat and fry the duck for 7–8 minutes, until the skin is crisp and flesh a little golden. Use a spatula to press lightly on the duck to flatten it to the pan, ensuring even cooking and a nice, crisp skin. Flip the duck over and sear for 20 seconds, then sear the sides for 10 seconds. Repeat with the remaining duck breasts until done.

Arrange the browned duck breasts on a baking tray and cook in the oven for 6–7 minutes. Take out of the oven and leave to rest for 10 minutes. Thinly slice the breasts diagonally and set to one side.

In a salad bowl, toss the sweet pea shoots, onion and cucumbers together, adding the tamarind dressing and tasting as you go. I like to add about 2 tablespoons of the dressing.

Dish the salad onto serving plates and arrange the duck slices on top. Drizzle over a final teaspoon of the tamarind dressing and sprinkle with crispy fried shallots.

Serves 4

- 4 duck breasts
- pinch of salt
- 200g sweet pea shoots
- 1 onion, thinly sliced against the grain
- 2 cucumbers, cut into fine matchsticks
- 1 tablespoon Crispy Fried Shallots (page 25), to serve

For the tamarind dressing
- 10g tamarind paste
- 100ml hot water
- 2 tablespoons caster sugar
- 150ml fish sauce
- 1 tablespoon finely chopped red chillies
- 1 tablespoon finely chopped garlic

For the spices
- 4 star anise
- ½ small cinnamon stick
- 2 tablespoons coriander seeds
- 2 cloves

Lemongrass Beef Noodle Bowl

Bún Thịt Bò Xào Sả Ớt

This dish is all about the beef: tender centres with edges that are almost well done, all bursting with the wonderful flavour of lemongrass. This is my first choice when I get a really good cut of meat and want something fresh and light to accompany it.

Combine the beef and all the ingredients for the marinade in a bowl. Mix together well and leave in the fridge for a minimum of 3 hours, or ideally overnight. Take the beef out of the fridge 45 minutes before cooking to come up to room temperature.

Heat the vegetable oil in a large frying pan over a medium heat until it reaches 160°C. An easy way to tell when the oil is ready is to place a wooden chopstick into it – when bubbles form on the surface of the oil it is ready. Add the beef and stir-fry for 3–4 minutes until cooked through.

Bring out the biggest bowls you can find … you'll need them!

First, add a handful of bean sprouts to each bowl, followed by a handful of noodles. To each bowl add some carrots, cucumbers, baby gem lettuce and the fresh herbs. Top with the cooked beef, then pour over a generous amount of the fish dipping sauce. Finally, sprinkle with crispy fried shallots, crispy garlic and roasted peanuts.

Now tuck in like no one is watching!

Serves 5

1kg topside beef, thinly sliced against the grain into 5cm long strips
3 tablespoons vegetable oil

For the marinade
3 tablespoons finely diced red chillies
3 tablespoons finely diced garlic
3 tablespoons finely diced lemongrass stalks
2 tablespoons fish sauce
1 tablespoon soy sauce
pinch of salt
3 tablespoons granulated sugar
5 tablespoons sesame oil

To serve
400g packet vermicelli rice noodles, cooked according to the packet instructions
300g bean sprouts
2 large carrots, cut into fine matchsticks 5cm in length
3 cucumbers, cut into fine matchsticks 5cm in length
5 baby gem lettuces, finely shredded
300g mint, finely chopped
300g coriander, finely chopped
5 stems Thai basil, torn
5 stems dill, torn
300ml Classic Fish Dipping Sauce (page 28)
2 tablespoons Crispy Fried Shallots (page 25)
2 tablespoons Crispy Garlic (page 26)
2 tablespoons Roasted Peanuts (page 25), optional

Thuy's
Creations

Thuy's Creations

In Vietnamese culture, the women will traditionally be the ones who cook, whether it's in the market or at home for the family. Daughters are judged by the quality of the food they make and how it is presented. It has even been known to be a major factor in some marriage arrangements. In our culture, everything comes back to food and many a young Vietnamese girl, me included, will have been told that unless she learned how to make a good bowl of pho then she would never find a husband! As bad as that last sentence sounds, it was never said to intentionally subjugate, it was simply a fact for that generation. Whilst I am very pleased to see that things are moving in the right direction for women in Vietnam, it is still generally expected that they should learn to cook. And yet it is through cooking and creating dishes that Vietnamese women are most able to showcase their passion and skills, and in doing so, bring pride and standing to their families.

Growing up, I loved being with the women in the kitchen, all cooking together and sharing in the preparation of the dishes. These kitchens were where women bond and friendships are made. It was a really special place with a sense of community and comfort. Everyone there was made to feel like part of the immediate family, even if they were just visiting friends or distant cousins. Grandma was the 'head chef' and we all had responsibility for a certain dish or ingredient prep. I think it's due to this experience and upbringing that I now treat everyone in my kitchen like they're family.

My experiences as a child in Vietnam and a young immigrant in London have no doubt shaped me and made me who I am today. I am determined, driven and very passionate (as my husband will no doubt tell you in a perhaps more colourful way!), and for me, failure is never an option. I've seen hardship in my life and, along with my family, faced struggles and times where we were literally wondering where the next meal would come from. Thankfully, though, I've been blessed with an amazingly close family who have always been there, looking out for each other. As a constant through it all, my mum has been an incredible role model for me: her determination has taught me how to be strong; her kindness has taught me how to care; and her passion has taught me how to love. She has shown me how to work hard and make the most of what you have in life, and it is for her that I try my best to live up to that example each day.

In my life I have learnt that you need to adapt and change according to circumstances, and I think that's true of our food too. Authentic Vietnamese food doesn't need to be traditional. The mantra of my kitchen is 'sometimes traditional, always authentic' and it's one that I work to every day. The methods and skills passed down to me by my mum are clearly present in every dish I send out of my kitchen; likewise the ingredients and flavours of Viet food are in everything I ever make. Many dishes in Vietnam are considered sacrosanct and even the slightest deviation can cause an outcry. Even for dishes that are cooked differently up and down the country, each province will think that theirs is the best, 'right' or even only way to do it (despite the fact it should be obvious to everyone that my mum's way is best!).

With this in mind I feel that it is time that we take Vietnamese food to another level! Play around with the traditional dishes and give them a twist or two: experiment with the techniques and ingredients to see where it takes you! This is what I've tried to do in this chapter.

The passion and creativity of the Vietnamese women in my life have inspired the recipes in this chapter: this is my homage to them. My dream is for my dishes and everything I do at The Little Viet Kitchen to help raise the profile of our delicious cuisine. I hope that along the way I can change some perceptions of Vietnamese food and get more and more people to fall as madly in love with it as I am. Every dish I serve and every recipe I design is an expression of my love and respect for my culture and heritage, and a way to bring my memories back to life and onto the table in my own unique way.

I hope that these recipes bring a taste of home to Vietnamese people living elsewhere in the world. To everyone else, I simply want to shout about our food and promote it as much as possible! So even if you never get to eat at The Little Viet Kitchen, I hope that you can take these recipes, bring the flavours of Vietnam to your table and, if only for the day, turn your kitchen into a little Viet kitchen.

Lemongrass Sa Tế Baked Cod Fillet

Cá Tuyết Nướng Sa Tế Ớt

Any white fish will work for this dish, but cod has always been my favourite pairing with sốt sa tế, chilli and lemongrass marinade. The meat is delicate in flavour and texture with a subtle sweetness that allows the kick of the sauce to really infuse into the meat. There is something so beautiful about seeing the deep red sauce seep into the clear white cod and knowing how it will come bursting through on your first bite.

In a small bowl, combine the ingredients for the marinade together well. Place the cod fillets on a plate and pour over the marinade. Lightly and carefully rub the marinade into each fillet, making sure they are evenly covered. Leave in the fridge for a minimum of 3 hours, or ideally overnight. Take the fish out of the fridge at least 45 minutes before cooking to give it a chance to come up to room temperature.

Preheat the oven to 180°C/160°C Fan/Gas Mark 4. Place the fish fillets, along with their marinade, and Asian shallots on a baking tray and roast for 10 minutes, until cooked. Use a fork to pierce the fillets gently; if it slides through easily then they're done, if not, leave for a further 4 minutes.

Now you're ready to serve. Share the roasted shallots between 2 serving plates and place a cod fillet on each. Drizzle with extra chilli and lemongrass marinade if you have some extra.

You can enjoy this dish as a refreshingly light dish on its own or with rice as a main course. I always recommend serving this with a delicious stir fry too, such as my morning glory stir-fry (page 165) or Vietnamese garlic broccoli stir-fry (page 58).

Serves 2

2 cod fillets (250g each)
2 tablespoons Chilli and Lemongrass Marinade (page 21), plus extra to serve
8 Asian shallots, peeled and halved
Crispy Fried Shallots (page 25), to serve

Caramelised Salmon and Green Peppercorns

Cá Hồi Kho Tiêu Xanh

I've chosen to use a non-traditional fish for this recipe because I wanted something readily available that wouldn't compromise the authenticity of the dish. For me, salmon works wonderfully as the meat is perfectly moist with a firmer texture than white fish, and of course it's absolutely delicious!

Place the salmon fillets in a bowl, add the ingredients for the marinade, and mix together well. Leave to marinate in the fridge for 3 hours. Take out of the fridge 30 minutes before cooking to allow the salmon to come to room temperature.

Lightly scrape the marinade from the salmon. You are aiming to remove all the bits in the marinade without removing too much of the marinade sauce. Leave the salmon to one side and reserve the marinade for later use.

Heat the oil in a saucepan over a medium heat until it reaches 160°C. An easy way to tell when the oil is ready is to place a wooden chopstick into it – when bubbles form on the surface of the oil it is ready.

Add the green peppercorns and stir-fry for 1 minute. Place the salmon, skin-side down, into the pan and cook for 3 minutes until the skin is crisp. Flip the salmon over and pour in the marinade and coconut water. (Avoid pouring onto the salmon skin, otherwise it will lose its crispiness.) Keep the pan on the heat for a further 4 minutes until the salmon becomes sticky and golden in colour. Keep the ingredients moving during this process, as you don't want them to burn, but avoid moving the fish as this could cause the fillet to break apart.

Now you are ready to serve. Carefully transfer the salmon to bowls with a little of the cooking liquid. Sprinkle with the spring onion, chillies and shallots. This dish is best served with rice and/or a side of vegetables.

Serves 4

500g salmon fillets
1 tablespoon vegetable oil
100g green peppercorns
250ml coconut water

For the marinade

2 teaspoons finely diced garlic
2 spring onions, white part only, finely diced
2 tablespoons soft brown sugar
3 tablespoons fish sauce
3 teaspoons sesame oil
1 teaspoon Caramel Sauce (page 27)

To serve

1 spring onion, sliced on the diagonal
1 or 2 red chillies, sliced on the diagonal
Crispy Fried Shallots (page 25)

Tuna, Mango and Pineapple Ceviche

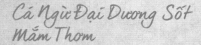

Cá Ngừ Đại Dương Sốt Mắm Thơm

This is another favourite from the Little Viet Kitchen's supper clubs. A light and delicate dish with an explosion of signature Vietnamese flavours. Quick and easy to make, yet looking — and tasting — sophisticated and complex. Not one to miss.

Similar to the lime-cured beef carpaccio (page 204), the secret to this dish is in choosing the highest quality ingredients. So skip a latte or two and spend it at the fishmongers instead. I promise it will be worth it.

Add the sugar and hot water in a bowl. Stir until dissolved and then add the fish sauce and lime juice. Set aside for 10 minutes to completely cool down.

Add the remaining salsa ingredients to the bowl and mix together well.

Arrange the tuna slices on small serving plates and top with the salsa. Now, did someone say wine?

Serves 4

500g sashimi grade tuna loin, cut against the grain into 0.5cm thick and 5cm long slices

For the salsa
2 tablespoons caster sugar
20ml hot water
150ml fish sauce
juice of 3 limes
60g pineapple, finely diced
¼ unripe mango, peeled, destoned and flesh finely diced
1 tablespoon finely diced garlic
1 tablespoon finely diced coriander stalks
1 tablespoon finely diced red chillies
1 tablespoon finely diced lemongrass stalks

Sea Bass, Passion Fruit and Blood Orange Ceviche

Cá Vược, Chanh Dây Và Cam Đỏ

Simple, sophisticated elegance on a plate. The only problem with this dish is that one portion is never enough.

First, you will need to supreme the blood orange. This is a little tricky to do but essential for this dish. Start by slicing off the top and bottom, just enough to expose the segments. Now, cut the peel off following the contour of the fruit. Make sure to get all of the pith off while being careful not to cut into the fruit too much. Now cut the segments out of the blood orange by slicing close to the membrane on each side. Repeat for the whole fruit and set aside. Now squeeze out all the juices from the core and combine this juice with the juice of the other blood orange for the sauce.

In a bowl, mix all the sauce ingredients together and stir until the sugar has dissolved.

Add in the cubed sea bass and gently toss together.

Spoon the sea bass and the dressing onto a serving plate, then lay on the blood orange slices. Sprinkle with the crispy fried shallots and micro herbs and you are ready to serve.

Serves 4 as a starter

1 blood orange
4 sea bass fillets, skin off and cut into thin slices on the diagonal, about 3–4cm long
2 pinches of micro coriander or coriander leaves

For the sauce
juice of 1 blood orange
juice of 1 lime
4 passion fruit, flesh scooped out
2 tablespoons fish sauce
2 tablespoons caster sugar
1 tablespoon finely diced red chillies
1 teaspoon finely diced garlic

Prawn Lollipops and Popcorn

Cây Kẹo Chạo Tôm

If I were to suggest one recipe from the book to make with your kids, it would be this one. It's both easy and fun to make, with lots of messiness involved (but easy to clean up). It tastes divine and is a great introduction to Eastern flavours!

Sometimes, I watch my sister force-feeding her kids and I wonder how it is even possible that they are not hungry? Dinnertime has been my favourite part of the day for as far back as my memory stretches. If you ask Mummy Pham, she will tell you that food even had to be hidden from me. Great-grandma knew my appetite (and charm of course) so well that she would always have three portions of treats: one for me, one for my sister and the third also for my sister after I bartered or stole her first.

I challenged myself to create something for my niece. Something fun, a little naughty but actually healthy, and something to introduce her to wonderful Vietnamese flavours. She loved it so much it made the restaurant menu and has been a huge success with kids and adults alike.

If this is for the kiddies then you may want to leave out the chillies… Or make them brave it out… Depends how mean you are I guess.

First, if using, make the mayo. In a large bowl, whisk the egg yolks and slowly add half the oil, whisking until the mixture has thickened. This will take either 5 minutes by hand or 20 seconds using a stick blender. Whisk in the rice vinegar and then slowly add the remaining oil, whisking until the mixture has once again thickened to the consistency of your preference.

Now add the chillies, lemongrass, crispy garlic, salt and lemon juice, and stir together by hand. (You can make this mayo in advance. It keeps for up to 2–3 days stored in an airtight jar and refrigerated.)

To make the prawn lollipops and popcorn, combine all the ingredients for the prawn mixture in a food processor and blitz for 25–30 seconds. Put into a large bowl and chill in the fridge for a minimum of 3 hours. For a perfect bouncy and ideal texture, leave the mixture in the fridge overnight.

Get all your rolling ingredients close to hand – that's the bowl of 3 tablespoons of oil, the bowl of breadcrumbs and the bowl of beaten eggs – and get ready to roll some lollipops.

Dunk 3 fingers into the oil and rub it over the palm of your other hand. Take a heaped teaspoon of the prawn mixture and roll into a ball about the size of a lychee. Dunk it in the beaten eggs, then roll in the breadcrumbs until evenly

Makes 40 balls

1 litre vegetable oil, plus
   3 tablespoons oil in a small
   bowl for rolling
300g breadcrumbs
4 eggs, beaten
40 lollipop sticks

For the Vietnamese chilli mayo (optional)

3 free-range egg yolks
375–400ml vegetable oil
1 tablespoon rice vinegar
1 teaspoon finely diced
   red chillies
1 teaspoon finely diced
   lemongrass stalk
1 teaspoon Crispy Garlic
   (page 26)
pinch of salt
juice of ½ lemon

continued on page 194...

coated. Place on a tray ready for frying. Repeat using about three-quarters of the mixture and leaving the remainder for the popcorn.

Heat 1 litre vegetable oil in a large saucepan over a medium heat and do the wooden chopstick test to make sure it is hot enough. Carefully drop one ball into the oil – this will be used to test your timings. Fry for 2–3 minutes, keeping the ball moving at all times using your chopsticks or spatula, until lightly golden and crisp. Remove with a slotted spoon and cool on paper towels.

If you are anything like me, you'll 'have' to eat this first ball. You know, just to make sure it's OK. This is your chance to adjust your timings to make sure the rest of the balls will be perfect.

Next, add as many balls as the pan can take at once, making sure that they don't touch. Again, keep them all moving throughout the frying process, cooking for 2–3 minutes, according to size, and removing to paper towels to cool.

To make the prawn popcorn, use just half a teaspoon of the reserved mixture and aim for a ball the size of a grape. For these, I'd recommend omitting the breadcrumbs to create a different texture to the lollipops – don't worry, both are equally delicious. Fry the prawn popcorn as per the balls for the lollipops.

To serve, simply thread 1 ball onto each lollipop stick. Tumble the prawn popcorn into a bowl and serve everything with a generous bowl of the Vietnamese chilli mayo.

For the prawn mixture

1kg prawns, peeled and deveined

2 tablespoons coriander stems, finely chopped

2 tablespoons carrots, very finely diced

1 teaspoon chilli, finely chopped

1 tablespoon crushed black peppercorns

4 spring onion stems, finely chopped

2 teaspoons granulated sugar

1 teaspoon salt

2 teaspoons fish sauce

3 tablespoons sesame oil

Pho-spiced Confit Duck with Soy-cured Duck Egg Yolks

Vịt Nướng Mỡ Và Trứng Vịt Ngâm Nước Tương

I wanted to create something that captured the prominent flavours of our national dish 'pho', but using Western techniques. Confit was the ideal choice for me as the meat is so soft and tender with a perfectly golden crispy skin, making that first bite just heavenly! So when combined with those beautiful pho flavours of star anise, cinnamon and coriander seeds it is absolutely delicious!

Mix the pho spice rub and the salt together in a small bowl.

Dry the duck legs thoroughly with paper towels, then thoroughly massage the rub and salt mixture into the duck legs, ensuring an even coverage. Place in the fridge to marinate overnight.

Preheat the oven to 150°C/130°C Fan/Gas Mark 2.

Take the duck legs out of the fridge and gently brush off the rub. Keep the duck away from any moisture – the purpose of overnight marinating is to extract all the moisture from the duck skin, ready to refill it with duck fat. Yes, it sounds awfully bad for you, I know, but that's what makes this dish so tasty!

Arrange the duck legs in a cast-iron casserole dish and pour over the duck fat, making sure it comes up at least 2cm above the meat.

Place in the oven and cook for 2 hours, then remove and leave to cool in the dish for 10 minutes.

Something useful to know… If you have any leftovers, the duck legs can be stored in the fridge for 6 months if you retain the fat.

Heat a large, dry frying pan over a medium heat. Take the duck legs out of the dish and place in the pan, skin-side down. Fry for 7–8 minutes, until the skin becomes crisp and golden. Turn and fry the other side for 10 seconds. Remove from the heat and keep warm.

Arrange the duck on serving plates and drizzle a teaspoon of the chilli and lemongrass marinade over each. Add a generous serving of rice with a soy-cured duck egg yolk placed on top, and a small handful of sweet basil, topped with the spring onion curls. Lastly, sprinkle over the crispy fried shallots and you are ready to serve.

Now, sit back and enjoy this fall-off-the-bone pho-spiced duck and wait for that silence – the moment of anticipation – at the table when people start to tuck in!

Serves 4

2 teaspoons Pho Spice Rub (page 21)
2 teaspoons salt
4 duck legs
2kg duck fat

To serve

4 teaspoons Chilli and Lemongrass Marinade (page 21)
4 Soy-cured Duck Egg Yolks (page 24)
4 handfuls of sweet basil
1 spring onion, finely shaved into thin curls
2 tablespoons Crispy Fried Shallots (page 25)

Crispy Courgette Flowers Stuffed with Lemongrass Prawns

Bông Bí Nhồi Tôm

When it's beautiful on the outside, and crazy delicious on the inside, what more could you ask for? This is an ever-popular chef's special at The Little Viet Kitchen. Make sure your diners are ready to be wowed!

Put the ingredients for the stuffing into a food processor and blitz for 25–30 seconds, until you have a rough paste. Tip into a large bowl and chill in the fridge for at least 3 hours. For perfect results, leave the mixture in the fridge overnight.

To make the batter, combine the flour with 250ml of water, stirring well until the flour has fully dissolved. It should be the consistency of double cream.

Take a courgette flower and add a teaspoonful of the stuffing mixture, leaving about a 2cm gap at the top. Close the flower by twisting the tip. Repeat this process for the remaining flowers and set the stuffed flowers aside on a tray.

Heat the oil in a saucepan over a medium heat until it reaches 160°C. An easy way to tell when the oil is ready is to place a wooden chopstick into it – when bubbles form on the surface of the oil it is ready.

Give the batter a little stir, then dip a whole stuffed flower into it. Carefully lower into the hot oil and fry for 4–5 minutes, dependent on size, until golden and crisp. Repeat for the remaining flowers.

This dish is great served as a starter with the classic fish dipping sauce (page 28), but also wonderful as a side dish in a traditional Vietnamese sharing meal.

Serves 5 as part of a meal of many sharing dishes or 2–3 as a starter

150g plain flour
15 courgette flowers, stamens
    removed
500ml vegetable oil

For the courgette flower stuffing

300g prawns, peeled
    and deveined
1 tablespoon finely chopped
    lemongrass stalk
1 tablespoon crushed black
    peppercorns
3 spring onions, finely chopped
1 teaspoon granulated sugar
1 teaspoon Chilli and
    Lemongrass Marinade
    (page 21)
1 teaspoon fish sauce
1 tablespoon sesame oil

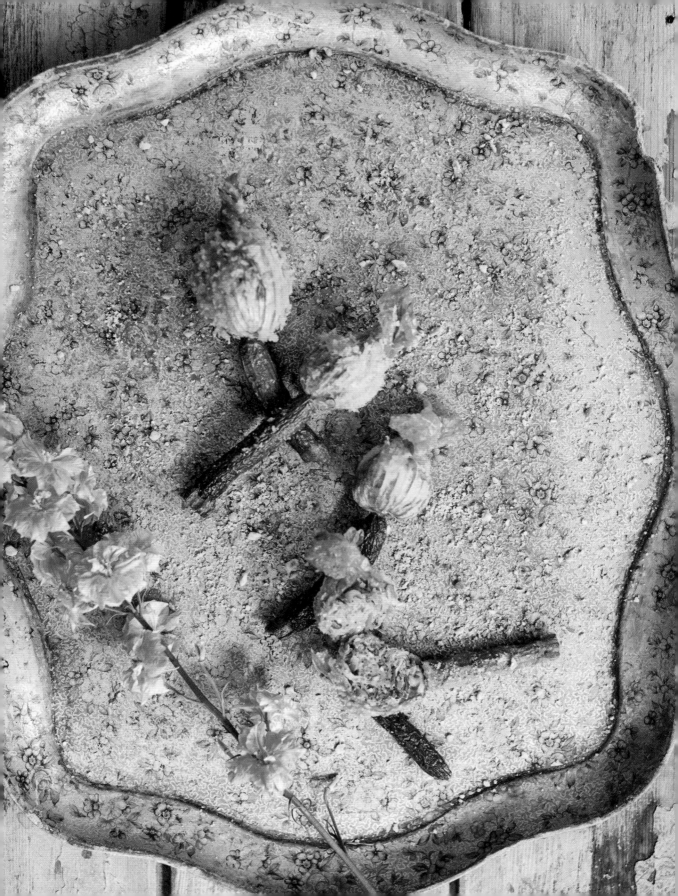

Tiger Prawn Tower

Tôm Tẩm Bột Chiên Xào Giòn

As you can probably tell by the name, this is an absolute show stopper. Juicy succulent prawns, bursting with Vietnamese flavours, it is definitely my kind of tower.

This dish can be served as a starter, part of a sharing platter or, if you love your rice like me, as a main with a bucket of classic fish dipping sauce (page 28). It is also a great option on a fresh salad noodle bowl.

Yummy, versatile and visually stunning, this dish is one of my all-time favourites to cook.

Put the prawns in a bowl. Line a baking tray with paper towels and put the cornflour in a bowl.

Heat the vegetable oil in a saucepan over a medium heat until it reaches 160°C. An easy way to tell when the oil is ready is to place a wooden chopstick into it – when bubbles form on the surface of the oil it is ready.

Lightly coat the prawns in the cornflour and carefully place into the oil. Deep-fry for 2–2½ minutes until the skin crisps and turns pink; the light batter coating will also become golden in colour. Repeat the process for the remaining prawns and place onto the baking tray.

Heat the annatto seed oil in a large frying pan over a high heat and do the wooden chopstick test if you like. Add in the ginger and garlic, and stir-fry for 2 minutes. Stir in the soy sauce and sugar and continue to cook for a further minute.

Add the chilli and lemongrass marinade, and the spring onions. Use your spatula to keep the ingredients moving around constantly for the next 30 seconds.

Now add the prawns, and stir-fry until every piece is coated in the seasoning. Take the pan off the heat and toss in the crispy fried shallots and crispy garlic.

Next it's time to build your jumbo tiger prawn towers. If by now you are not super-excited and hungry, then you're a stronger person than me.

Insert the sharp end of a bamboo skewer into the centre of the cut side of a lime half. Pierce right through to the other side and push through until the base of the skewer is level with the flesh of the lime. This will now be the base for your tower and it should be able to stand upright unaided. Now, take a prawn and slide it down the skewer. Aim for 3–4 prawns per skewer or go as high as you like.

Have your salt, pepper and lime dip in separate small bowls for each diner and tuck in.

Serves 6

12 raw jumbo tiger prawns, deveined, shells and heads left on
120g cornflour
500ml vegetable oil
6 bamboo skewers
3 limes, halved
Salt, Pepper and Lime Dip (page 27), to serve

For the seasoning
90ml Annatto Seed Oil (page 22)
60g finely chopped ginger
2 tablespoons finely chopped garlic
1 tablespoon soy sauce
1 tablespoon granulated sugar
4 tablespoons Chilli and Lemongrass Marinade (page 21)
3 spring onions, finely chopped
40g Crispy Fried Shallots (page 25)
40g Crispy Garlic (page 26)

Lime-cured Beef Carpaccio

Bò Tái Chanh

Here is a beautiful vibrant cut of tender beef fillet, so thinly sliced it almost falls apart at a touch. Sour, sweet, salty, spicy, soft and yet crunchy, this is the perfect dish to represent the Vietnamese palate.

It's probably my favourite salad and certainly the dish that gets the most praise from my supper club guests. It's also the one that I save for those special occasions when I really want to show off Vietnamese food. It's a little time consuming to prep, especially for a Vietnamese nhậu dish, but so worth the extra effort.

The truth is I don't make this dish often, but when I do, I will only use the finest fillet I can get my hands on. There is no other way for this one. It's such a delicate dish that you can really taste the difference of a better cut. It may cost more, but it's a real treat whenever you make it.

I can still remember the first time I ate bò tái chanh. I was excited but terrified at the same time. It's a traditional nhậu dish, which means it's only for adults, mostly for dad and his friends. I would hear the noises they would make when taking a bite, the compliments mum would get every few seconds. Being curious and ever hungry, I asked mum if I could taste a bit. She looked at me, not surprised but a little sad to have to burst my bubble. It was raw meat, she told me, and that's why it was only for adults. Not cooked? Well, that did sound scary. I know now that that's not completely true — the acid in the lime actually cures the meat a little — but the nine-year-old me was not to know this. Nevertheless, I decided to be brave and see what the fuss was all about.

I took a bite-sized portion onto my chopsticks, and placed my free hand on my chest, closed my eyes and in it went … my mouth exploded with the most amazing flavours. I didn't even notice the meat was raw — it just melted with kicks of herbs and spices, and the crunch from the peanuts offsetting the softness of the beef. Love at first taste you could say. I was so happy that I liked it. It made me feel like a grown-up. From that day on I would always flutter my eyelids at daddy to get a chopstickful, whenever it was available.

Over the years, I've added a few touches of my own to mum's traditional southern recipe and I'm thrilled to be able to share them with you.

Try to start making this when you're just about ready to serve. This way, the herbs and papaya will stay fresh and crisp. You want it from mixing bowl to belly in as short a time as possible.

continued on page 204...

Lime-cured Beef Carpaccio...

Put the ingredients for the marinade in a small bowl and mix together well.

In a rectangular dish, place a single layer of beef down flat, spreading the pieces across the base. Pour the marinade over the beef, then tilt the dish around to make sure that every piece of beef is coated. Leave the marinade to work its magic for 20 minutes while you prepare the rest of the meal.

In another bowl, mix together the coriander, onion, red chillies and lemongrass, and pour over the classic fish dipping sauce. Hand toss everything together, then divide between serving plates.

Remove from the dish and arrange the beef on top of the plates. Sprinkle over the spring onion and lime zest, and you are ready to serve. Put any extra garnishes in little bowls on the table so that diners can add more as they eat.

The taste of this dish is amazing but it can look amazing on the plate too. Have fun with your plating and your garnishes and create something you can be really proud of.

Serves 2–3

400g beef fillet, sliced thinly
   into 5cm pieces
1 tablespoon finely chopped
   coriander stems
1 onion, thinly sliced
2 red chillies, thinly sliced
1 tablespoon finely diced
   lemongrass stalks
150ml Classic Fish Dipping
   Sauce (page 28)

For the marinade
90ml lime juice
30g finely diced fresh pineapple
4 tablespoons fish sauce
2 tablespoons caster sugar
1 tablespoon finely diced
   red chillies
1 tablespoon finely diced garlic

To serve
1 spring onion, finely sliced and
   chopped to 5cm
lime zest, grated

Pan-seared Fillet of Sea Bass

Cá Chiên Xả Ớt

This is a simple and delicious way to enjoy fish. I would recommend serving this with a fresh salad or as a substitute meat on a noodle bowl, and you can find inspiration for these throughout the book. And served in a bánh mì (page 22) it is just to die for!

Place all the marinade ingredients into a small bowl and mix together thoroughly.

Lightly score the skin of the sea bass fillets, being careful not to cut into the flesh. Rub the marinade evenly across both fillets and leave in the fridge for a minimum of 30 minutes to marinate. For the perfect amount of flavour, and if you have enough time, I'd recommend leaving them for 3 hours.

Take the fish out of the fridge and leave to adjust to room temperature for 10 minutes or so before cooking.

Heat the oil in a frying pan (or saucepan) over a medium heat. An easy way to tell when the oil is ready is to place a wooden chopstick into it – when bubbles form on the surface of the oil it is ready.

Add the fillets, skin down, and fry for 3 minutes. Turn over and fry the other side for a further 2 minutes. The aim here is to crisp the skin while keeping as much moisture as possible in the fish, so don't over cook it! It should be crispy and golden brown on the outside, with the flesh white and not opaque.

Serve with a wedge of lime, delicious!

Serves 2

2 sea bass fillets, 100g per fillet
4 tablespoons vegetable oil
lime wedges, to serve (optional)

For the marinade
3 teaspoons sesame oil
1 teaspoon soy sauce
1 teaspoon fish sauce
2 teaspoons lemongrass,
    finely chopped
1 teaspoon garlic, finely diced
1 red chilli, finely diced

Coconut Braised Beef Short Ribs

Sườn Bò Kho Nước Dừa Và Trứng Vịt Ngâm Nước Tương

Your whole kitchen will smell of the beautifully balanced aroma of beef and spices when you make this dish. The beef, tender and flavoursome, melts in your mouth yet is still meaty and substantial. The hit of the spices is there on the bite and then softened and smoothed by the sweetness of the coconut.

When creating a dish, I am always aiming for that brief window of silence after the first mouthful. Growing up in a Vietnamese household, silence only happened when the food was too good for words. This dish always achieves that goal. Invite your noisiest friends over and watch the magic happen.

Season the ribs with salt, rubbing it in well. Set aside for 30 minutes.

Preheat the oven to 150°C/130°Fan/Gas Mark 2.

Heat 4 teaspoons of vegetable oil in a ridged grill pan over a medium heat. Add the ribs and sear each side for 1 minute. Remove and allow the ribs to rest for 5 minutes, while you prepare the marinade.

Place all the ingredients for the marinade in a large casserole pan and add the seared ribs. Cover with the lid and braise in the oven for 4 hours.

To plate, place some short ribs next to a generous portion of fluffy jasmine rice, topped with a soy-cured duck yolk. This dish is best served with a side of vegetables or a fresh green salad.

Serves 4 as part of a meal of many sharing dishes

4 beef short ribs, approximately 250g each and as meaty as possible
2 teaspoons salt
4 Soy-cured Duck Egg Yolks (page 24), to serve

For the marinade
2 litres coconut water
6 star anise
1 cinnamon stick
3 lemongrass stalks, halved and bashed
3 red chillies, halved lengthways
4 tablespoons fish sauce
4 tablespoons granulated sugar
½ teaspoon salt

Green Peppercorn Steak

Thịt Bò Hạt Tiêu Xanh

It is fairly uncommon to find beef cooked rare in home-style cooking in Vietnam. There are a few exceptions of course, most notably pho, and also generally in nhậu dishes such as beef carpaccio or duck's blood salad.

However, living in London for most of my life, surrounded by a fantastic variety of amazing restaurants, I have learnt to appreciate the delicate flavours and textures of a great cut of meat cooked rare.

The recipe here is inspired by that Western style of cooking meat, yet it captures essential Vietnamese flavours to bring together the best of both worlds.

Preheat the oven to 200°C/Fan 180°C/Gas Mark 6.

To make the green peppercorn glaze, heat the sesame oil in a small saucepan over a medium heat until it reaches 160°C. An easy way to tell when the oil is ready is to place a wooden chopstick into it – when bubbles form on the surface of the oil it is ready.

Add the garlic, lemongrass and green peppercorns and sauté for 3 minutes. Add the soy sauce and sugar, then cook for a further minute, stirring at all times as the sugar is likely to burn at this stage if you aren't careful. Add the chillies, take the pan off the heat and set the pan aside.

Place the tomatoes and shallots on a baking tray, drizzle over the olive oil and roast for 10–12 minutes, until the tomato skins have split and are bursting with juices.

Divide the beef into 2 portions and rub a pinch each of salt and crushed black peppercorns onto both sides of each piece.

Heat the vegetable oil in a frying pan over a high heat. Do the chopstick test and, when the oil is hot, add the beef to the pan. (The following timings will vary depending on the thickness of your beef fillet so adjust timings accordingly.)

Sear the beef for 1 minute, turn over and sear the other side for a further minute. Repeat with the sides. Immediately remove the beef from the pan and allow to rest on a chopping board for 5 minutes.

Start plating by dividing the watercress between serving plates. Top with the roasted tomatoes and shallots. Drizzle with the fish sauce and lime salad dressing.

Once the beef has rested, slice against the grain into 1cm thick strips. Arrange the beef beside the salad on the plate and finish with a drizzle of the green peppercorn glaze.

Serves 2

12 cherry vine tomatoes
8 Asian shallots, peeled
    and halved
3 tablespoons olive oil
500g beef fillet
4 pinches of salt
4 pinches of crushed black
    peppercorns
2 tablespoons vegetable oil
200g watercress, washed
    and drained
1–2 tablespoons Fish Sauce and
    Lime Salad Dressing (page 28),
    to drizzle

For the green peppercorn glaze

4 tablespoons sesame oil
1 tablespoon finely diced garlic
1 tablespoon finely diced
    lemongrass stalk
150g green peppercorns
4 tablespoons soy sauce
2 tablespoons granulated sugar
1 tablespoon finely diced
    red chillies

Sweet
Treats

Sweet Treats

Dessert isn't something we tend to have at the end of a meal in Vietnam, instead it is more often a treat, either as street food or as part of a celebration, like a wedding, a birth or at Tết (New Year). You'd very rarely have them at home on a normal day. In the run up to Tết the women of the household will spend many hours preparing the sweet dishes for the celebrations. It is a wonderful time with lots of conversation and laughter. For me, a huge part of my love for Tết comes from these happy times bonding with my family.

At Vietnamese weddings, dessert is a large part of the celebration. The sweetness of the dishes represents the sweetness of the relationship and the hope for it to continue into the marriage. All the guests will then share in the eating of these dishes as a way of wishing the couple luck and joy in their future. Traditionally the groom's side will give a gift of fruit and cakes to the bride's side as a welcome to the bride and as a symbol of good will between the families.

In Vietnam, how we make dessert is really a celebration of life. The ingredients used are often picked because they sound similar to something positive, like the giving of papaya and mangoes together. Papaya in Vietnamese is đu đủ and mango, xoài, and when said together it sounds like đủ xài, which means having enough money to spend comfortably. Other times the dish itself will have meaning; xôi is eaten during Tết as the stickiness of the rice represents friendships and relationships sticking together for the year to come. Other desserts and sweets are coloured red or gold, symbolising good luck, happiness and fortune.

All through Vietnamese culture sweet things like fruit and desserts tend to be more about the gesture than the actual eating. They are personal dishes, often loaded with meanings that can say far more than words alone. There is something about the giving of food that makes it more than it is; it's symbolic and so full of love. My great-grandma would take a fruit from the tamarind tree, coat it in sugar and wrap it up for us as a homemade sweet. She used to say that the fortunate person always has someone to give something too. This little piece of wisdom will stay with me forever.

As a child I would know that something good was happening when a dessert appeared on the table, so for me, desserts and sweet things will forever inspire happy memories. Food always tastes better when you're happy, and this is never truer than with Vietnamese desserts, as these sweet dishes are so bound up in good memories. One of the vendors at our local market sold chè bắp (sweetcorn and coconut pudding). My sister and I would always run up to her when we were at the market, excitedly hoping that we'd be allowed a bowl. I can still remember the joy we would have on those rare occasions when mum would smile, nod her head and allow us to ask auntie for some. This was a real treat, as it meant that mum had sold all of her eggs the day before and we had a little money spare. I looked forward to these days, and because it was such a rarity, I think I enjoyed it all the more. The sweetness and creaminess of the coconut and sweetcorn, contrasting with the crunchy and salty peanut topping, is still something that I crave to this day.

Desserts and sweets in Vietnam are generally made from simple flavours, unlike our savoury dishes, which are packed with contrasts and intense flavours. Desserts tend not to be overly complicated, although each region has subtle variations in their recipes and methods.

In this chapter you will find the recipes that I grew up with on the Mekong Delta. They are the dishes that my mum made for me, and grandma made for her when she was a child. I hope they bring you as much joy and as many memories as they have done for me.

Sweet Ginger Mung Bean Dumplings

Chè Trôi Nước

A traditional New Year's treat in every Vietnamese household, this dessert is a firm favourite thanks to the delicate balance between savoury and sweet that Viet palates love. The spicy ginger kick is an added bonus.

Soak the mung beans in a large bowl of cold water for 30 minutes. Drain.

Make the ginger sauce. Bring 45ml of water to the boil, then add the sugar and crushed ginger. Stir until the sugar has dissolved, then take the pan off the heat and leave to cool. The consistency should be just slightly thicker than water.

To make the dough, put the flour and salt into a large bowl along with 450ml of cold water, mix together well and set aside for later.

Put the mung beans into a saucepan with 750ml of cold water and bring to the boil. Immediately reduce the heat to low and simmer for 20–25 minutes, until the mung beans become very soft and almost all of the water has reduced down. Keep an eye on the beans as they can burn very easily. Remove the beans from the pan and set aside in a bowl.

In a small saucepan, combine the oil, salt, spring onions and desiccated coconut. Sauté for 1 minute, take the pan off the heat and add the mixture to the cooked mung beans. Stir everything together well.

Take the dough mixture and create a disc on the palm of your hand, around 7cm in diameter and just 0.5cm thick. Add 2 teaspoons of the mung bean mixture to the centre of the disc. Turn the edges in towards the centre and seal the dough, making a ball roughly the size of a golf ball. Pinch off any excess dough as you are aiming for a smooth and even consistency around the ball without any gaps.

Repeat this until you run out of filling mixture. Then start making some deliciously addictive marble-sized dumplings without any filling. These are seriously tasty.

In a medium saucepan, bring 1 litre of water to the boil. Add a few dumplings to the pan, making sure that they don't touch, and allow to boil for approximately 5 minutes. When the dumplings appear translucent and float to the surface of the water, they're ready.

Repeat the process for all of your dumplings, both big and small.

Serve one large ball and a few mini ones per portion. Dress with 2 tablespoons of the ginger sauce and 2 tablespoons of creamy coconut custard.

Now sit back and enjoy the dumplings with friends or, if you're feeling greedy, eat them all yourself!

Makes 24

For the ginger sauce
200g soft brown sugar
50g ginger, grated

For the dough
450–500g glutinous rice flour
½ teaspoon salt

For the filling
150g dried mung beans
1 tablespoon olive oil
½ teaspoon salt
½ spring onion, green part
  only, sliced
20g desiccated coconut

To serve
400ml Creamy Coconut Custard
  (page 27)
Roasted Peanuts (page 26),
  crushed

Steamed Banana and Coconut Cake

Bánh Chuối Nước Cốt Dừa

If you like bananas then you'll love this delicious cake. The sweet-savoury Vietnamese twist of creamy coconut custard works beautifully on this dessert too … although I have such a soft spot for coconut custard that I would happily pour it over almost anything!

Put the bananas in a large bowl and add the sugar, salt and vanilla extract. Mix together and set aside at room temperature for 30 minutes. The natural sweetness of the ripened bananas will merge with the rest of the ingredients and release a beautiful aroma that will make you start to salivate for the cake already.

Add 400ml of water and the tapioca flour, and mix well until the flour has completely dissolved.

Take a 23cm round cake tin and grease the base evenly with the butter. Pour in the cake mixture. A little bumpy layer of banana popping up is what you are after so don't feel you need to press it down and make it neat.

Have your steamer ready, and bring the water to the boil. Place the tin in the steamer, put the lid on and lower the heat to a simmer. (Alternatively, use a large saucepan filled partially with water. Sit the tin on a tripod inside the pan, making sure it doesn't touch the water.) Steam for 20 minutes, checking back after 10 minutes to carefully pat dry the lid where condensation has formed. (You want to avoid any moisture falling onto the cake.) Be patient and keep the heat low. High heat will force the cake to rise quickly but the cake will then deflate and end up much worse for it. Not a bad metaphor for life, huh?

Carefully remove the tin from the steamer. The cake should be pale in colour with a slightly translucent appearance. Insert a toothpick or skewer into the centre of the cake and if it comes out dry and clean the cake is ready. If not, return to the steamer and give it another few minutes.

Allow the cake to cool fully before cutting and remember to 'grease' your knife with cold water when slicing. Traditionally, this cake is served in a diamond shape, but you're the chef and it's your cake, so cut it as you please.

Serve drizzled with warm coconut custard and sprinkled with sesame seeds.

Makes 1 × 23cm cake

1 teaspoon butter, to grease

For the cake mixture
500g ripened bananas (about 3 bananas), peeled and cut into 1cm slices
60g soft brown sugar
pinch of salt
1 teaspoon vanilla extract
220g tapioca flour

To serve
Creamy Coconut Custard (page 27), warm or at room temperature (optional)
1 tablespoon roasted white sesame seeds

Sweetcorn and Coconut Pudding

Chè Bắp Nước Cốt Dừa

Sunshine in a bowl! The bright yellow sweetcorn seems to almost call out my name whenever I pass a vendor selling this. Perhaps it's because it was such a rare treat as a child, but I don't think I've ever managed to walk by as an adult without indulging!

Soak the mung beans in a bowl of cold water for 1 hour. Drain and set aside.

Crush the peanuts into small bits using a pestle and mortar. Make sure you only break the peanuts up, being careful not to turn them into a paste. They need to add texture and crunch.

Use a sharp knife to shave the kernels off the corncobs. Make the shavings as thin as you can. You should get approximately 3–4 layers around each corn. When you get close to the base of the kernel you'll notice the resistance to your knife increase. Stop at this point, as including this part of the corn will add an unpleasant chewy texture to the dessert. Set aside the corn shavings for later.

Heat the mung beans and coconut milk in a saucepan over a medium heat and cook for 25 minutes. Add the chopped corn along with the tin of coconut cream and leave to cook over a medium heat for 15–20 minutes. It's ready when the beans are nice and soft so start tasting after 15 minutes and take the pan off the heat when the pudding is done.

Serve divided between small bowls garnished with desiccated coconut.

Serves 6

250g dried peeled mung beans
1 tablespoon Roasted Peanuts
   (page 26)
6 corncobs
3 × 400ml tins coconut milk
400ml tin coconut cream
200g granulated sugar

To serve
400ml Creamy Coconut Custard
   (page 27), warm or at room
   temperature (optional)
1 tablespoon desiccated
   coconut, roasted

Black-eyed Pea Pudding

Chè Đậu Trắng

This is a simple home-style dessert that mum would often make at the weekends. She always preferred for us to eat treats made by her so she knew exactly how much sugar was in them. It wouldn't stop my cravings for chocolates and sweets of course, but oh my, a bowl of mum's black-eyed pea pudding will always get a thumbs up from me!

Soak the rice in a bowl of cold water for 1 hour. Drain.

Heat 1 litre of water in a saucepan and bring to the boil over a high heat. Add the rice, cover with the lid and reduce the heat to low. Simmer for 30 minutes until soft and the texture of thick porridge. Add the beans and sugar, and stir well. Take the pan off the heat and divide the pudding between glasses or small bowls.

Drizzle with the creamy coconut custard and sprinkle with roasted peanuts.

Serves 6–8

200g sweet glutinous rice
400g tin black-eyed peas,
    soaked in hot water for 5
    minutes and drained
50g coconut palm sugar

To serve
400ml warm Creamy Coconut
    Custard (page 27)
1 tablespoon Roasted Peanuts
    (page 26)

Sesame Mung Bean Lollipops

Bánh Cam

The beauty of these is you can really make them any size you want. I often make them huge when it's for just me but quite small when they're for party nibbles, as kids love them!

First, make the dough. Place all the flours, the baking powder and oil into a large bowl. Mix together well and set aside for later.

Heat 200ml of water and the salt and sugar in a small saucepan over a medium heat and stir until the sugar has dissolved. Take the pan off the heat and allow to cool for 30 minutes, then add to the dough mixture.

Knead the dough until it is soft and smooth with no bumps, then set aside to rest for at least 3 hours. It will rise slightly and dry a little which will help to make it easier for the moulding later.

Soak the beans in a large bowl of cold water for 1 hour. Drain.

Put the beans and 250ml of cold water into a saucepan and bring to the boil over a high heat. Immediately reduce the heat to low and simmer for 20–25 minutes, until the mung beans become very soft and almost all of the water has reduced down. Keep an eye on the beans as they can burn very easily.

Take the beans out of the saucepan using a spoon and set aside in a bowl. Add the salt and 2 tablespoons of water and mash everything together. You are aiming for the texture of mashed potatoes so add more water if needed.

Now it's time for the fun part… Let's make some balls!

Take the dough and make a disc on the palm of your hand about 0.5cm thick and 5cm in diameter. Add a teaspoon of the bean filling to the centre of the disc. Turn the edges in towards the centre and seal the dough, making each ball about the size of golf balls. The key is to avoid any gaps in the dough.

Repeat the process until all of the dough and filling has been used. Roll the balls in the sesame seeds, ensuring a good even coverage.

Heat the vegetable oil in a saucepan over a medium heat until it reaches 160°C. An easy way to tell when the oil is ready is to place a wooden chopstick into it – when bubbles form on the surface of the oil it is ready.

Add as many balls as you can manage at once, making sure that they don't touch. Fry the balls, keeping them moving at all times, for 8–9 minutes depending on their size. The idea is to wait until the balls puff up and turn a delicious light golden colour.

Place the cooked balls on paper towels to drain any excess oil and allow to cool and then thread onto lollipop sticks. Happy eating!

Makes 24 balls

1 litre vegetable oil
250g white sesame seeds
24 lollipop sticks

For the dough
225g glutinous rice flour
120g rice flour
50g potato flour
1 teaspoon baking powder
1 teaspoon olive oil
½ teaspoon salt
110g granulated sugar

For the filling
150g dried mung beans
¼ teaspoon salt

Index

acknowledgments

From as far back as I can remember, a beautiful and delicious dish will always make me very happy and a home cooked meal by my mum will fill not only my belly but also my heart. Now as a cook myself, an empty plate brings me more joy than it probably should. So the idea of filling the bellies of a hundred hungry strangers each night and passing on that joy has always been a dream for me.

The launch of my restaurant The Little Viet Kitchen was the realisation of that lifelong dream, and the satisfaction and happiness it gives me each day is the most priceless of rewards. Doing what I love allows me to give my all, willingly, openly and with no hidden agendas. It allows me to put passion and care into the tiniest of details and the littlest of things that matter only to me, and hopefully now to you too.

However, the reality that comes with this dream requires an awful lot of hard work to be done each and every day. No one can do all that alone and I am so fortunate to have the most wonderful and supportive family around me to help with the long hours and hard graft. It has been an amazing experience and more than I had ever wished for to be able to share my love affair with food with you through this book; but none of it could have happened without these very special people in my life.

In the aftermath of the Vietnam War, my father felt that to give his children an education and the opportunities that this brings, his only option was to risk his life at sea. So thank you Ba for opening doors for me that I would never have even known existed without your act of extreme bravery and love. I hope I've made you proud.

My mother means everything to me and whilst I struggle to express this adequately in words, I will try. She is my mentor and my inspiration. Everything I am as a chef she has either taught or influenced. She has been there for me at every single step of my life, pushing me forward but ready to catch me if I was to fall. Thank you Mẹ for being my chef, my toughest critic and for making me the person I am today.

The unsung heroes of The Little Viet Kitchen are my siblings, Pastry Chef Hanh Kasperuk, and Sous Chef Anthony Pham. Your hard work and tireless support not only keeps the restaurant going, but on so many days, is essential for keeping me going!

Dave Kelly, my husband and business partner. Thank you for believing in my crazy ideas and visions; dreams and goals that no one else would ever understand. Your love makes me strong, your faith in me pushes me forward and with you by my side, I know nothing is impossible!

To my nieces Eva and Lara, and my nephew Lucas, you are too young to understand just how much you mean to me but your unfiltered and unconditional love never fails to pick me up on even the hardest of days and the joy you bring to my life is absolutely priceless.

My biggest fan and loudest supporter, my mother-in-law, Mummy Kay. Your unfailing support and excitement at even the tiniest success is always, always appreciated. Thank you.

To Jon Croft, my forever charming and debonair publisher. Thank you for having faith in me and for inviting me into your family. You have been a calming influence and stalwart throughout. I couldn't have asked for anyone better to guide me through the journey of this book.

credits

Publisher Jon Croft
Commissioning Editor Meg Boas
Project Editor Emily North
Art Director & Designer Marie O'Mara
Food & Prop Styling Thuy Diem Pham
Photography David Loftus
Copyeditor Kate Wanwimolruk
Home Economy Elaine Byfield
Proofreader Margaret Haynes
Indexer Zoe Ross
Florist Sarah Davey, Kitchen Garden Food and Flowers

Cover shoot location
deVOL Kitchens, London (devolkitchens.co.uk)
Hair Styling (cover) Kieron Lavine
Make Up (cover) Sergio Alvarex Gonzalez
Thuy's t-shirt (cover) Ted Baker
Thuy's skirt (cover)
Mirror Mirror Couture (mirrormirror.uk.com)
Meat supplier for photoshoot
HG Walters (hgwalters.com)
Vietnamese producer for photoshoot
Longdan (longdan.co.uk)

ABSOLUTE PRESS
Bloomsbury Publishing Plc
50 Bedford Square, London, WC1B 3DP, UK

BLOOMSBURY, ABSOLUTE PRESS and the Absolute
Press logo are trademarks of Bloomsbury Publishing Plc

First published in Great Britain 2018

A catalogue record for this book is available from the
British Library.

Library of Congress Cataloguing-in-Publication data has
been applied for.

ISBN: HB: 978-1-4729-3603-5
         ePub: 978-1-4729-5643-9
         ePDF: 978-1-4729-5642-2

2 4 6 8 10 9 7 5 3 1

Printed and bound in China by C&C Offset Printing Co.

Bloomsbury Publishing Plc makes every effort to ensure
that the papers used in the manufacture of our books
are natural, recyclable products made from wood grown
in well-managed forests. Our manufacturing processes
conform to the environmental regulations of the country
of origin.

To find out more about our authors and books visit www.
bloomsbury.com and sign up for our newsletters.